For The Silent

An anthology to aid the work of
League Against Cruel Sports

Indigo Dreams Publishing

First Edition: For The Silent
First published in Great Britain in 2019 by:
Indigo Dreams Publishing Ltd
24 Forest Houses
Halwill
Beaworthy
Devon
EX21 5UU
www.indigodreams.co.uk

ISBN 978-1-912876-04-4

British Library Cataloguing in Publication Data. A CIP record for this book can be obtained from the British Library.

Designed and typeset in Palatino Linotype by Indigo Dreams.

Printed and bound in Great Britain by Imprint Academic, Exeter.

Papers used by Indigo Dreams are recyclable products made from wood grown in sustainable forests following the guidance of the Forest Stewardship Council.

We would like give huge thanks to Richard Bowler for kindly allowing us to select a photograph as the cover image. Richard is a UK based wildlife photographer passionate about the natural world. He hopes his images inspire people to protect the wonderful environment around us.

Richard has a particular love of foxes and feels very privileged to care for three, Rosie, Hetty and Charlie. Together with his terrier Maddy they have appeared in the national press and in features and stories around the world, hopefully changing opinions on foxes, to an animal they wish to protect.

His images are represented by RSPB images, Cover images and Rex features.

https://www.richardbowlerwildlifephotography.com/
Richard is also on Twitter and Facebook

About the Editor

Ronnie Goodyer is an experienced poet and publisher. He is a director of Indigo Dreams Publishing which he runs with his partner, Dawn Bauling. IDP publishes poetry collections, anthologies, and three poetry/prose magazines. It also runs competitions for prizes and publication. IDP was a winner of the Most Innovative Publisher category in the annual Saboteur literary awards and Ronnie and Dawn were the first joint winners of the Ted Slade Award for Services to Poetry.

Ronnie ran his own Celebrity Management company and published Uri Geller's first novel *Shawn* and also England cricketer-turned artist Jack Russell's *A Cricketer's Art*. He was invited to be on the BBC Judging Panel for their *Off By Heart* competition. aired on BBC2.

Ronnie has six solo collections and is currently working on a new joint collection with partner Dawn.

A strong supporter of animal rights and the natural world, Ronnie is extremely proud to be Poet-in-Residence for the League Against Cruel Sports

He lives with Dawn and their rescue blue merle collie Mist in an ex-forester's house in the rural southwest of England.

Indigo Dreams and the League Against Cruel Sports would like to thank the following supporters for their wonderful contribution to the creation of this anthology.

Andy Allan

Elizabeth Allison

Maggie Baptiste

Dawn Bauling

Angela Bell

Gillian Beviss

Brian Blackwell

Janet Burt

Joan E Carter

Janis Clark

Kay Cotton

Jacqueline Deeks

Sarah Emmett

Stella Fenwick

Margaret Fielder

Vivien Foulkes-James

Annest Gwilym

Jenny Hamlett

Stephen Hartley

Pamela Trudie Hodge

Judith Kaye Howard

Dr Wendy Hudson

Annie Maclean

Kathy Miles

Tina Negus

Jan Moran Neil

David Norris-Kay

Jan Oswick

Terry Quinn

Pamela Radford

Carol Robb

Jill Ross

Barbara E. Robinson

Chrys Salt

Simone Stanbrook-Byrne

Judith Stevens

Peter Geoffrey Paul Thompson

Linda Tilbury

Marilyn Timms

Patricia Wickham

Mick Yates

The League Against Cruel Sports

The League Against Cruel Sports is Britain's leading charity working towards a kinder society where persecuting animals for sport is in the past.

Redefining what is acceptable and inspiring change, we were instrumental in helping bring about the landmark Hunting Act (2004), which banned hunting with hounds in England and Wales. Yet sadly, we are still having to fight to protect animals from illegal hunting which takes place far too often across the UK.

Driven by compassion and empowered by knowledge, we manage sanctuaries to protect wildlife, carry out investigations to expose law-breaking and cruelty to animals, and campaign for stronger animal protection laws and penalties.

The League receives no government funding and relies entirely on the generosity of its supporters.

We would like to take this opportunity to say thank you for supporting us by buying this anthology. We ensure you that every penny really does count in helping us to protect animals from being harmed or killed in the name of sport. United, we can redefine what is acceptable and give animals the voice they deserve.

Indigo Dreams, the publishers of *For The Silent*, have kindly undertaken this venture with and to benefit the League through a Charity Partnership Agreement with profits being paid to the League from each book sold. It is the first anthology in our 95-year history, so very important to us. We would like to express our thanks to them for suggesting and bringing this to life and to the

League's Poet-In-Residence **Ronnie Goodyer** for his hard work and dedication as Editor.

If you'd like to get involved further in our work or learn more please visit www.league.org.uk or call our Supporter Care Team on 01483 524 250 or email supportercare@league.org.uk

Thank you for supporting us by purchasing *For The Silent*.

With kind regards
Andy Knott MBE, CEO
and all at the League.
United, we will end animal cruelty in the name of sport.

A few words from the Editor...

When I suggested this idea to the League, and they agreed, I was wondering what response I would receive from poets when details were released. 'Overwhelming' would probably be the answer! It took me three months to go through the submissions and decide which poems would give the quality and variety I was seeking. The hardest part of the selection process was writing to people who obviously felt passionately about the cause but were not accepted. The response I received from those poets was encouraging and understanding, their support for the book undiminished.

It was never intended that the poems in *For The Silent* would all concern the cruelty that animals suffer. I wanted to embrace the beauty of wildlife, address other factors that affect animals. There are some that hit you in the face, others that perhaps enlighten and show how the world could be; there is everything from a butterfly to a whale!

Whatever the subject matter, the embracing factor is that everyone wished to contribute to the success of this book because of their love for animals and animal welfare, their loathing of cruelty and because they believe in the work of the League Against Cruel Sports. No animal should shed blood for 'sport'.

Finally, all those whose work is included in *For The Silent* and those who granted permission for use of work, have given their time, energy and talent free of charge for the benefit of the League. We would like to applaud and thank each one of you.

~ Ronnie Goodyer

"Of course writing a good poem is impossible, if what you want is one which holds infinite raw readings. I make do with echoes, live for an echo of whatever poetry is. It's my religion, that, and animals. Animals are of course pure poems, but we only perceive their echoes."

~ **Pascale Petit**

CONTENTS

For The Silent

JOHN SADLER

Inglorious Twelfth – Ronnie Goodyer

The day has finally arrived.
Factory farms have despatched to estates,
the cramped cages emptied, the fate
of the grouse is being sealed where money swears.

The moor has been burnt,
the snared fox gone, the harrier, the crow
are missing. The records will show
the mountain hare was slaughtered for just cause.

The feathered targets are wary.
Beaters bellow fear into grouse to fly
into butt-concealed guns, the sky
filled with terrified life, then gunshots and death.

The moor is now scarred
with carcass. Life that began cramped and caged
has ended in death for 'sport', waged
for the thrill of killing: Glorious killing.

The Huntsman Wants To Kill – Ronnie Goodyer

The golfer wants a hole in one
The cricketer to score a ton
The sprinter to be number one
The huntsman wants to kill

The footballer to win the league
The cyclist to avoid fatigue
But the huntsman wants none of these
The huntsman wants to kill

Ignore the child-on-pony pose
For cameras at country shows
Beneath the pomp and pompous clothes
The huntsman wants to kill

Called from the Field, the vilest trade
Is carried out by men with spades
Their presence proves this grim charade
The huntsman wants to kill

The hounds are seen to run in packs
On busy roads and railway tracks
There's no 'trail' here – it's just a fact
The huntsman wants to kill

To flush a fox and watch it run
Is his idea of perfect fun
Content when violent death has come
The huntsman's had his kill

We'd educate him if we could
No sport should ever call for blood
Enforce the ban, so that, for good –
The huntsman cannot kill

The animals in that country – Margaret Atwood

In that country the animals
have the faces of people:

the ceremonial
cats possessing the streets

the fox run
politely to earth, the huntsmen
standing around him, fixed
in their tapestry of manners

the bull, embroidered
with blood and given
an elegant death, trumpets, his name
stamped on him, heraldic brand
because

(when he rolled
on the sand, sword in his heart, the teeth
in his blue mouth were human)

he is really a man

even the wolves, holding resonant
conversations in their
forests thickened with legend.

> In this country the animals
> have the faces of
> animals.

Their eyes
flash once in car headlights
and are gone.

Their deaths are not elegant.

They have the faces of
no-one.

Fawn, drinking – Sharon Larkin

Fresh-faced Narcissus came to the water's edge
and looking down, immediately fell, infatuated.

Not so this nimble-footed fawn, gentle tongue
touching the water, barely rippling the surface.

I note the reflection, the double loveliness,
know this young deer has come just to drink
not to preen in the sheen of this shallow pool,

I hold my breath as I scan the wider scene,
expect to see his mother, sibling, or a future
mate – but no, this Bambi lookalike's alone.

Scarcely daring to move, I'm slow to align him
in the cross-hairs, close focus on his left eye,

feel my forefinger first tremble, then squeeze
the cable-release for the prize-winning shot.

Man the Hunter – Oz Hardwick

For I haf hunted al this day, and noght haf I geten
Bot this foule fox felle – the fende haf the godes! –
            — Sir Gawain & the Green Knight *(late 14ᵗʰ c.)*

Blood-daubed, you tell me man
is a hunter – always has been,
always will be. It's in the genes,
a trait of the tribe, the need to provide,
the need to protect, a call to the wild
beneath tamed land, tamed lives.

So you run with your pack in scarlet coats,
a snarl in your throat, a beast bellow
harsh in your breast, questing hounds
snorting at the ground, sweat and spit
flecking flanks and faces, eyes
squinting in the wind against the rush

of an age that's left you far behind,
shoring up your self-importance
with flayed flesh, bones as exposed
as naked hate, as you gloat at the blood
dripping from a useless carcass, the pride
of your tribe in tatters, thrown to the dogs.

Badgers – Anna Saunders

We almost miss what looks like a junked rug
with a black trim, heaped on the side of the road.

The badger is coiled foetal, harlequin face
tucked under a paw, white lines
running over its head like road markings, pale belly
peppered with stones.

It's still breathing, and dad calls wildlife rescue,
as we wait by the animal, pat its springy fur.

Dehydration we are told later,
The roads a desert if you're wearing fur.
In the background we hear the badger scampering.

The next family holiday we see another -
opened up as if for heart surgery,
glossy red ribbons spilling out onto the road.

My dad makes another call and the soft body,
an arrow to the sett, is removed
before the badger baiters can bring their dogs
to make sport with the animals that remain.

I only remember this, years later, the same night
I see a fleshy mound on the side of the road,
a glistening snout, a small paw protruding
like a hand reaching out for alms.
A badger, I think, briefly, without slowing down.

From *Burne Jones and the Fox,* Indigo Dreams Publishing 2016

The Fox – Simon Armitage

Standing its ground on the hill, as if it could hide
in its own stars, low down in the west of the sky.
I could hit it from here with a stone, put the torch
in the far back of its eyes. It's that close.

The next night, the dustbin sacked, the bin-bag
quartered for dog meat, biscuit and bone.
The night after that, six magpies lifting
from fox fur, smeared up ahead on the road.

First published *CloudCuckooLand,* Faber 1997
Copyright © Simon Armitage 1997. Reprinted with permission of
David Godwin Associates Ltd, London, on behalf of Simon Armitage

Laughter of Slaughter – Rebecca Gethin

He preferred to shoot elephants
from behind trees, not in open ground
but up here in the mountains
elephants fed on grasslands.
No trees. Different tactics required.

He chased them on horseback
considered it sportsmanlike and fair
to stand in the way of danger
just a bit, so he'd shoot females
in the forehead as they charged him
in defence of their young
leaving their *poonchies* alone to starve.

He loved the frisson of kill,
seeing the creature buckle and fall,
admiring the straight accuracy of his bullet,
the feel of a newly loaded rifle being placed
in his grip by his Ceylonese gun-bearer.

He rejoiced to see herds of elephants rotting
in his footsteps, called all of them *rogues*,
described the Lankan elephants
with their pale speckled faces *disgusting*.

'On my return to the village I took a shot-gun and strolled along the
banks of the lake. The snipe were innumerable, and I killed them till
my head ached with the constant recoil of the gun in addition to the
heat.' *The Rifle and the Hound*, Sir Samuel Baker, 1853. He murdered
more than 3000 elephants.

Syke – Kerry Darbishire

Cumbrian
rhymes
with dyke
grike
and even if
you're blind
you can
hear it
in the shade
of willow
hazel
ash
a line
thin
slower
than a beck
a bark
a place
to hide
drink sky
cool tongues
lose scent
lead a fox
to safety

Ghost of Southall Horse Market – Eve Jackson

By now they will all be dead, but little ghosts of grief
will not let me forget. How some out-lived themselves:
long-toothed, sway-backed, broken-winded, arrived
baulking, jibbing and traffic-shy, hung out to dry
on a rack shaped to what they once were.

Wednesday Lots came - and some would always come
again. Lathered and leathered, water not offered,
elbowed and jostled the long day; jumping,
twitching to the clatter and din.

Long-coated men, fusty with years of haggling,
would spit on their palm and pull at a wad of notes
clamped in a golden tongue. I once bought one
and saved none.

End of day with animals and crowds towed away
a wide broom drags an old man through the empty stalls.
Mizzle of rain moans on corrugated roofs. My dream
that each horse was once blessed with some tenderness.

This market continued for nearly 400 years. The treatment of horses
did, over time, improve a little.

Myths of the Fireflies – Matthew Friday

At night a single tree
in the Puting Najing National park
lights up with buzzing magic:
the fireflies gathering to tell stories
as they dance the darkness
sparkling like a shower
of fizzling stars filling up
the spiraling black holes of night.

The true stars rise above Borneo,
souls of ancestral dancers, elevated
to delight Mother Moon
while she shies away from
The King of Flies, her bright
suitor, so bright, no fly can dance
while he owns the heavens,
searching for her, east to west.

All night they dance, playing
at being Stars, Mother, Father
in their home on a glue-green river
in a forest of rain-drenched diversity
being hacked into tinier and tinier
chunks by palm oil plantations.
During the day they hide in the reeds
while trees fall and Mother weeps.

The Bag – Sheila Aldous

The Red Grouse lies low,
his call a warning for her to stay
in what is left of burnt heather,
to not follow whatever happens.

She looks for his handsome eye,
his red cap, his feathery claws;
in grey shadows she hides
in the moorland hollows.

She will know him, his scent blown
on a glass mist, his red stripe
that makes him hers,
the strength of his wingbeats.

At first light she will hear him
rise up, leave swift and low;
he will not heed her warning
to *go back, go back.*

She will yield to the moss
crouch down in the upland bog,
wait his return, his cackling call,
hide from the shooters.

Even in the blaze of the rising
sun, he will refuse a blindfolded
eye to armed men intent on a kill,
as he flies towards their fire.

At the beaters' whistle
she too will lift herself up,
speed to the wave of flags
towards the line of guns.

And when the small bores
are spent, spent with fun money,
she will rest again in wait for him
shrug off the stain

the stain of what she is to them,
sink into the slough of
the shooters' inglorious bag,
into her silence.

Spirits of the High Weald – Jane Lovell

(i) Hare

Early morning air
slice-cold below total blue,
and he's sitting, bold as a stray, on the lawn
tasting the breeze, absorbing every ripple
with those planetary ears.

Time passes only in the shiver of leaves,
a solitary beetle ticking in the sage.

In a heartbeat, he's away to the skyline
unzipping the grass and wind-chased verge
giving us the whole month of May
stretched languorously through centuries,
myrtle, mint and purple betony,
twirling her skirts
shaking her hair in the wind,

gathering speed as if in huntdown,
as if pinning the lawn with his longbone feet,
bursting through streamers of birdsong,
scattering like confetti the trimmings
of finch and sparrow,
carrying his ears so beautifully,
so beautifully,
all the way to the furthest corner

where he pauses,
resting on his haunches
in the lee of a budding lilac

and breathes,
breathes the whole sky:
invisible worlds,
distant constellations,
pared-down moon.

(ii) Vixen

and there
through this Japanese ghost garden
this monochrome dreamscape
slips a half-dreamt wraith

born from the last shades of dusk
she is tip tip toeing on footfall so soft
it uncurls snails
dizzies galaxies in dew

her vagabond heart
beats with the tremors of the earth
balances on owl call
and the breeze rushing the trees

behind her swim timorous worlds
we can never enter

so slight and swift she moves
that without the moon billowing through
the cherry and all the fallen blossom
luminous as snow
I would not see her

Repeated Patterns – Annie Maclean

*'every year approximately 20 million pheasants are reared … released …
and brought down by the shooting community.'*[1]

Her ancestors knew the eastern shores
dense scrublands
and the grasslands
where they raced the Black Sea's breezes
before becoming migrants
carried by the Greeks to Europe
to cross the Channel with the Romans
holding hopes. Scattered seeds.

On the new land
capture and commercial breeding.
The fairytale became the nightmare
when, shocked and terrified by beaters,
they were forced to fly across a clearing
where a line of guns gunned down their line.
And the massacres kept on repeating.
If the dead could not be hung for meat,
the carcasses were heaped and buried.

Where flies the value of a life?

A secret plan was hatched by keepers
that all the nightingales be shot
to let the pheasants sleep at night. [2]

Broody hens joined into harems
to flitter, camouflaged, in woodlands.
Stripey. Calm. And looking kindly.

and

uselessly
the strutting males
stared blankly
behind their bright red goggles.
Bodies glowing.
Long feathers trailing –
already promised as a present
to decorate a sweetheart's bonnet.

[1] and [2] Cocker M. and Mabley R. (2005) *BIRDS BRITANNICA*, Chatto & Windus

The Running of the Deer – Denise Bennett

Born with the love of land
and animals, my uncle,
a gentle lad of Exmoor,
hated to watch the hunt;
loved to see the red deer running free.

It wasn't easy then, he said.
When I worked for the Squire
I had to run with the hounds
or lose my job.
There were younger brothers and sisters
at home to feed.

At the end of the chase
when the stag ran exhausted
tired, torn and bleeding,
he would stop his ears…

Years later, unfettered,
he wrote endless letters
to the newspapers campaigning
against this cruel blood sport –
thoughts of white spotted fawns,
of hinds grazing a dawn,
the majesty of the stag,
always in his heart.

Blodeuwedd – Jean Atkin

A woman in a caul of owls
walks feather-naked in the dark.

She hunts the oak wood,
sings beneath her breath.

She's pliable as saplings,
scents layers of fur and blood.

At every stride the owls' eyes ripple
with her moony flesh

and round her they rotate
their hungry heads

and snap their beaks so field-voles
bolt and freeze.

She cannot stop. She cannot feel
the thorns. Benighted she

cannot recall the golden broom
and meadowsweet of day.

From *Not Lost Since Last Time*, Oversteps Books in 2013.
Blodeuwedd is the wife of Lleu Llaw Gyffes in Welsh mythology. She
was made from the flowers of broom, meadowsweet, and oak by the
magicians Math and Gwydion, and is a central figure in the last of the
Four Branches of the Mabinogi. But later Gwydion turns Blodeuwedd
into an owl, the bird hated by all other birds, in vengeance for her
betrayal of her husband to her lover Gronw.

The Hunt – Matt Duggan

Twenty eight pairs of eyes
chase moving amber
over pockets of broken snow;

I always believed that sport was supposed
to be gauged by two equals;
for strength and agility not an army verses one.

The men that ride in red through winter streams
corked by the sun are the emblematic reasons
why I retreat from any form of patriotism.

They harness the empirical nature of a darkness that lingers
in the cygneous cracks of a country's neck;
that once spread into its lungs to voice privilege and class division;

Twenty eight pairs of eyes chase moving amber –
over pockets of broken snow.

Blue Hare – Elspeth Brown

A snow-blended hare has been shot.
He lies in the heather, panting, eyes terrified,
fur turning white before the snow, now bloodstained.
It is a cull, they say, WE need to control the numbers.
WE need to manage the grouse moors.
HE doesn't watch the Blue hare die, as his ears fall
and eyes close with a shudder.

The Bull Fight – Shanta Acharya

*Man is the cruellest animal. At tragedies, bullfights, and crucifixions he
has so far felt best on earth; and when he invented hell for himself, behold,
that was his very heaven.*
Friedrich Nietzsche, Thus Spoke Zarathustra

Men in costumes march ceremoniously into the arena –
a grand entry to the triumphalism of a *paso-doble.*

Foot followers draw the bull's attention as he charges in
nostrils flaring, mouth foaming, disoriented –

released from his dark prison, blinded by the light.
Spectators cheer, indifferent to the bull's plight.

No sign of the saint's compassion, just the travesty
of the matador's flourish to display his skill –

wide red cape performing the *Verónica* sweeping
close to the bull's face as the saint wiped Christ's.

These wild bulls raised on the vast ranges of Andalusia
are chosen for their *tienta,* their bravery.

Yet these prize fighters do not stand a chance against
picadores mounted on horses padded, blindfolded, sedated.

Ready with pikes the lancers plunge their weapons
into the bull's neck and hide until he staggers in pain, bleeding.

In the last act the matador with sword in his right hand,
muleta in his left, thrusts the sword into the bull's heart.

Death is not instant, the bull is left standing like a hero
heaving, brightly coloured little flags trembling like medals

on his shoulders – *banderillas* marking man's inhumanity,
bearing witness to the barbarism of human beings.

A second bull is dragged away, bleeding from the ring.
The crowd goes wild as the third charges in.

A Mighty Grouse – Roz Allen

Beyond the wild north borders on blooming heather moors
game birds are amassing to sharpen beaks and claws,
there's fire in their hearts, dark thunder storms the skies,
beware the raptor rattle of their crowing battle cries.
The message is quite clear, their leader Rory Red
has groused on Twitter networks and here is what he's said.

'It's an outrage that we noble and superbly handsome birds
are hunted just for sport, there truly are no words
to describe the gruesome carnage of our fear-foul situation
when you blast us with your guns causing callous devastation.
The killing fields are red with the blood of kith and kin,
annihilated, decimated – what a shocking sin.

I hear our cousin pheasants are reared in metal cages,
I've heard their distant pleas, I've felt their frantic rages.
You have a bloody taste for partridges and duck,
the geese have all migrated, I ask you 'what the pluck?',
Would you like it if we shot you then butchered you for tea,
or left you maimed and wounded when once you wandered free?

So, we'll fight you in the mountains, we'll fight on nesting grounds
we'll fight you in the hedgerows and your dogs we will impound.
We've enlisted sniper armies, we've honed our flying power,
Our stratospheric fleet will form a mighty tower.
Feathered with destruction we'll commandeer our skies
and when we're feeling peckish, we'll feast on people pies'

Tanzanite – Fokkina McDonnell

Gemstone found in Tanzania

Slices of life extinguished,
rough at the edges, almost round.
They can be turned to face the other way.
In this shiny polished slice animals
may be buried: a crocodile, a baboon.

*

In the cold eye of a hunter
slices of time are captured.
In the eyes of a dying animal
the whole world is reflected.

The Song of Sally Weaver – Zoe Mitchell

When I change from woman to hare, I shrink
but am never diminished. It's freedom,

I feel it keenly; the close-packed power
of muscles made to run, the speed that feels

like flight and the joy of a barefoot streak
across close-cropped turf and deep green valleys.

Over the downland in my brindled pelt,
I race along the belly of a whale.

Only romance can trap me; my lover
can confiscate my charm if I confess.

All my magic would drain away, the crunch
of spring-loaded rules would shatter my bones.

I am careful not to let any man
love me but even if I dart away

there are other means of capture – hunters
and predators will soon find the scarpfoot

and the moon isn't always a mother
to us all. She can light a gun sight too,

she's as much a friend to the stalking hounds
as she is to me. I must keep moving

to be free. If I am shot, I wonder
where the bullet goes, which creature it kills.

As both woman and hare I ask nothing
of the world than that I may run and know

the grassy hills, the sea and sky, the fossils
and bands of flint that sleep beneath my feet.

From *Hag* Indigo Dreams, 2019 reprinted by kind permission of the publisher

To Those That Defy the International Ban on Whaling – Jane Burn

A space of sea
as big as four million cars,
two million houses,
twelve million men.
Great brained, huge-headed, pottval –
named for a boiled creature.
Oiler of industry. Please, not sperm.
Call her Cachalot, after her teeth,
this wonder, rather than after what we took.
Scrimshaw scratched, to pass the time –
pictures of ships, portraits of loves ones.
Words. Try Physeter
and bring to mind her blowhole, her breath.
Even her iron-rich shit
grows the creatures that eat
the carbon from our air.
She is magic.

Sixteen months to grow her baby inside her.
It will drink one hundred gallons of milk in a day.
Each will carry tonnes of blood in their veins.
Big enough to sink the *Essex*.
Big as a bus.
You could fit the weight
of two human beings
inside her heart.

Old Fox – Gill McEvoy

Beneath the thinning stars of early dawn
a horse and rider forge the dark.
The old fox trains his mind on them,
reads the signals in their smoke of breath,

sharpens the pencils of his ears
to hear the clang of trailer ramps,
the bell-cold peal of foxhounds
clear as spoon on glass.

No-one sees him quit
his snuggery of leaves,
snorkel down a stream
four fields' length of chill.

He climbs out, shakes himself
then lopes away, not hurrying,
mouth half open in a kind of grin.

First published in *The Plucking Shed* Cinnamon Press, 2010

Night Hare – Denise Margaret Hargrave

A
shy hare
her soft fur
bristling with life
jumped down from the moon
with moonlight in her eyes
onto a summer meadow
zigzagging among shadows
of the wind. Electric
in the night air, she
returned my stare
pricking up
pointed
ears.

Largesse – Hélène Demetriades

An owl
heavy with moon
swoops
dusting the earth
with feather tips

She rises glowing
carrying
the breadth of the world
between her wings

CountrEcocide – Geoffrey Winch

"Whenever men allow their minds to
forsake the sweet sanity of the earth,
there is danger."
Llewelyn Powys: The Cradle of God

England's lovely mosaic of meadows,
forests, fields – shaped over centuries
by sweat and toil – and for centuries
haunted by baiters, stalkers, hunters
satisfying their primal lust for blood.

Ancient science of seeding by rotation
to produce wholesome yields – now,
through science, land being poisoned
by insect-and-herbiciding transforming
our acres to prairie-fields.

Hedgerows once cut, woven and laid
by skilful hands – the nesting-places
and pleasures of stock-proof greenery
now flailed into submission
by men's machines.

Eco-friendly ditches and waterways
annually re-dug, trimmed, maintained
by hand to be free-flowing – now
backfilled, ploughed-out or left
to silt stagnating fertile soils.

Greenbelts of natural habitats, rural
living and employment, farms for
food, and our recreation – lovely
landscapes fast becoming developers'
all-for-profit havens.

Yet that which has survived of our
lovely meadow, forest and field mosaic
remains still the haunt of baiters, stalkers
and hunters persistent in their savage
quest to spill scarlet blood.

Sky Dancer – Lorna Faye Dunsire

Our moorlands are graced with a rare stunning sight,
where swirling above is a raptor in flight;
those lucky to see face fewer delights.

Whirling and turning the sky dancer display.
The female is brown, the male white and grey.
Aerobatic parade that takes breath away.

But this beautiful vision you're unlikely to view:
for now these Hen Harriers are fewer than few.
So many nests empty the sky's lacking too.

The moorland and heather irresponsibly burned-
destroying the habitat with no wildlife concerns.
On the edge of extinction you'd think that we'd learn.

These incredible birds are now on the brink
of being wiped from our moors with no time to re-think.
It's enough to make any really wild heart sink.

So why are their numbers so greatly depleted?
Robbed of this beauty, all nature is cheated-
as they poison and shoot these irreplaceable creatures.

Where shooting of grouse is seen as a thrill;
inglorious game, she plummets, then still.
They sacrifice our nature for their cold-blooded kill.

This great British cause now needs strong support;
to stop birds disappearing from protected resorts.
It's abhorrent and wrong that this goes on today:
That they kill all our raptors to hunt all their prey.

So soar with the raptor and accept this brave quest;
to roar now for nature and allow it to nest.
Only then, will we see our land at its best.

Leverets – Kate Innes

Huddled in a form, midfield,
their only protection from hawk and fox
is immobility and earth-brown fur.
Wide eyes can see the approach
of their doe or death equally well.

They are too small yet to learn
how to dodge and run;
how to make their hearts pump
power into legs, stretched
to launch the arrow of precarious life.

The hare bursts from the grass, runs,
switchback, tangling her scent trail.
The form is not a nest;
she suckles them sitting up.
Ear tips twitch. Nose dilates.

It may be a distant buzzard's call;
the stink of a vixen in the wind.
The leverets are still – perhaps they sleep,
briefly reassured and full.
She will go now, before they wake,
running before the talon, tooth and wheel.

Playing Fetch in Fog – Carl Griffin

If I lived this far in the sticks
I would jump off Overtoun Bridge
just like the dogs
which have leathered off it in frenzies

fetching a stick nobody threw.
It's the bridge
we've come to visit,
not the barony beyond. The central arch

spanning the deep valley,
the decorative bartizans and rough-
faced ashlar. And its river gorge,
its mass canine grave.

Where there is mystery
there are theories—
scent of mink, sonic effects
in the bridge structure—

but only dogs jump here,
dogs with long snouts,
in clear weather,
from one side of the bridge but not the other.

We dare not jump
even to conclusions.
If the unseen force was named
we would not think to explore.

The gun was one thing – Carole Bromley

securing its case to the wall,
removing the bullets,
lying to the kids about its purpose.

Now here you are, the rain
the only sound on this Scottish moor
and you on your belly, wriggling.

How gentle the doe is,
nervously testing the air
which carries no scent of you.

In your sights now,
she pauses to flinch off a horsefly,
lowers her head to the heather.

Last Rites – Jenna Plewes

The bright yellow digger rumbles slowly up the hill, missing her by inches. The driver yells at her. There's no pavement on this stretch of road, so where is she supposed to go. She struggles on past the blank-faced houses with their unforgiving windows. The wind blows a strand of grey hair into her eyes and she pushes it back with her free hand leaving a smear of blood down her cheek. She adjusts her grip in the broken thing knocking against her thighs and stops to ease the pain in her chest. Her heart drums in her ears and she lifts her chin. Out of the corner of her eye she sees a curtain twitch. Let them think what they like; it's no business of theirs. She strides on, shoulders back, head held high.

The young woman lets the curtain fall, and turns to her husband. 'She's got another one. She's weird, it's not as if she's poor. That big house must be worth thousands. It's sick, in my opinion, eating road kill. Puts me right off my breakfast.'

At the top of the hill the old lady pushes open the gate, and makes her way slowly round the house into the back garden. She lays the young fox gently on the grass and goes to get her spade. The sun touches the glossy pelt. She starts to dig. A gust of wind shakes the hazel catkins, yellow pollen dusts her shoulders, drifts into the grave.

The Fallow Deer at the Lonely House – Thomas Hardy

One without looks in tonight
Through the curtain-chink
From the sheet of glistening white;
One without looks in tonight
As we sit and think
By the fender-brink.

We do not discern those eyes
Watching in the snow;
Lit by lamps of rosy dyes
We do not discern those eyes
Wandering, aglow
Four-footed, tiptoe

Such Savagery – Anne Harding

(on hearing that the Hunting Act of 2006 could be repealed)

She sleeps wrapped in her mother's smell,
Unseeing, but safe in the womb-like earth,
Close by she feels the movement of other bodies,
 A bark and her mother sniffs the air,
Stealthily the dog fox enters with his kill,
Allowing the vixen to eat her fill.
Vixen and dog lead the cubs into the world,
They must learn to hunt.
Galloping hooves, new sounds to her ears,
Earth becomes hell as teeth grip her throat,
Red the colour of her blood, of her death.
Should such savagery return?

Published in *Quaker Concern for Animals Newsletters*

Tasting the Wild Grapes – Mary Oliver

The red beast
who lives in the side of these hills
won't come out for anything you have:
money or music. Still, there are moments
heavy with light and good luck. Walk
quietly under these tangled vines
and pay attention, and one morning
something will explode underfoot
like a branch of fire; one afternoon
something will flow down the hill
in plain view, a muscled sleeve the color
of all October! And forgetting
everything you will leap to name it
as though for the first time, your lit blood
rushing not to a word but a sound
small-boned, thin-faced, in a hurry,
lively as the dark thorns of the wild grapes
on the unsuspecting tongue!
The fox! The fox!

Against the Garden – Oak Ayling

Bodies slumped
Between tires and tarmac
Bless my children, Lord
Boys know badgers
By the colour of their dead
Broken by the weight of progress

See how we have turned against the garden and its growth?

How many horses, four? With their
Hundreds of hooves pounding, thunder
Hide! Hide! Hide!
Here come the white, red, black, pale
Horses, Horsemen, Hounds and foaming
Hound's teeth, 42 daggers bared, baying
Hear the sound of the world ending for one
Hear the sound of us marching to our own

See how we have turned against the garden and its growth?

Bless the wings of
Birds which will not carry them to safety
Bow your heads for a hundred thousand
Bodies falling softly to the ground
But the season is the season; feathers, ash will rain down, Oh
Bloodlust is it's most savage in the civil.

See how we have turned against the garden and its growth.

Shooting the greys – Alwyn Marriage

Bristling with privilege and whiskers,
he was leaning conversationally on his 12 bore

and sporting, despite warm autumn
weather, tweed jacket, collar and tie.

Pests he spat, indicating a sickly
ring-barked chestnut tree;

while high above, a drey swayed cheekily
hiding and protecting a future generation.

He looked kindly, smiles twinkled in
his eyes; on his tie the motif of a red

squirrel; on his hands blood
from shooting the greys

Published in *The Broadsheet*, 2013 and *Pop Up Anthology* 2014

three haiku – Alan Spence

sheer exhilaration -
three dolphins leaping
out there in the bay

sweetening, sweetening
my evening meditation,
the blackbird's song

old dog in the rain
yawning -
seen it all

Carved by the Wind – Bridget Thomasin

Carved by the wind
out of rock, time
is a vixen's cry tearing
the darkness, this night
    and forever

Waking – Bridget Thomasin

Rain at last.
 A fox fiery bright
roams unquenched the sodden fields
of a soaked and shining world.

With the rain
 the cuckoo's long awaited
cries burst through the emptiness
of dry grey days.

and deep in the valley deer
inhabit the dripping trees
shadowing the paths to secrecy.

River Mink – Zoë Sîobhan Howarth-Lowe

Fishing at a twist of water;
a river running through red clay.

Waterlogged afternoon,
feet dangling,
waterbirds dipping into mud-suck -
water-swirls feathering out
and noises hinting from weeds.

Water swirls around bare toes, the water-dippers ascend
clamouring upwards as the surface breaks -
a sodden-fur head
brown and lithe
cylindrical.

Staring after the startled birds then turning
eyes to my eyes
inquisitive.
Sliding out onto the banks

fur bounding through weeds
pawprints across wet clay
performing for the fish I haven't caught.

Do I feel lucky? – Ann Drysdale

I came across a slow-worm in a wood.
I saw it clearly but a little late,
making me have to stumble-jump aside
so that I wouldn't put a foot on it.

The dog peered at it, but with little more
than passing interest in a fellow-creature.
I picked it up to move it off the path,
thrilled by the feel of it, smooth in my hand.

I took delight in the blunt head of it
pushing between my fingers; the dry slide
as it dripped from the safety of my grasp
and took possession of the ground I gave it.

I put leaves over it; it thrust its head
up into daylight from a space between them.
I blessed it with a single fingertip
and it ducked down and drizzled out of sight.

It was a lucky day for pseudo-snakes.
What if another poet had been there?
Lawrence, for instance, with a log to hand,
might have made short work of its loveliness.

A different woman with a different dog,
a squealer with a killer, might have made
a noisy and uncomfortable end
of the uncomplicated innocent.

It seems the end of everything depends
upon which agent of apocalypse
steps from the shadows when the chips are down.
Saviour or slaughterer. Call heads or tails.

I will spend no more time on hedging bets.
Bring on the Rapture when the time is right.
I'll take my chances, knowing as I do
the arbitrary nature of salvation.

Is there life after death? – Darren Beaney

Yes...
You die and come back

as:

An elephant killed for a pair of ivory cufflinks.
A mink bred to keep some rich bitch warm.
A bull tortured by the matador – "OLE!"
A maggot impaled on an anglers hook.
A rabbit wearing lipstick and blusher.
A snail squashed by a spiteful child.
A fox ripped apart for Sunday sport.
A dog whipped by a callous owner.
A rat born with man-made cancer.
A fly exploding on a windscreen.
A dolphin choking in a tuna net.
A hen laying in a battery farm.
A veal calf boxed on a plane.
A spring lamb in the abattoir.
A tiger hunted to extinction.
A slug attacked by salt.

Yes
       you die

             and come back...

Haunting your soul.

Two Fawns – Eileen Carney Hulme

Don't be afraid
trees have hearts
and this forest
is your home
no one owns you
here, now
at the edge of morning
ephemeral
as the muse
graceful
as the moon
and sun
slow dancing
in a startle of blue.

Sea Raven – Doreen Hinchliffe

on the back of the tallest cliff
a green-eyed cormorant stands alone

beyond the reach of spume and foam
tossed up from sea-splashed rocks

he spreads wet wings   holds them aloft
hangs them out to dry in the gathering wind

the slap and swerve of air bends
and batters the long curve of his neck

as he tilts his head far up   far back
his yellow throat stark against a charcoal sky

like some dark angel robed in black and grey
he views the arc of the revolving world

the sheen on his feathers flecked with gold
in the flickering embers of a winter sun

content   he sinks into quiescence   musing on
deep-sea diving and the maundering of hapless fish.

Big Game – Caroline Maldonado

In a few minutes he'll pose
on one knee behind the corpse,
baring his teeth for the camera,
rifle by his side, but first he reaches
to stroke the soft fur on its belly,
the angular haunches
sculpted for speed.

He curls the mane
through his open fingers,
flattens his hand against
the neck - still warm
though the breath is gone,
the flesh won't rise under his palm
and the dark open eye can't see him.

They've Shot Our Stag – Stephen Reneaux

It matters not
Who fired the shot.
But I do wonder, why?
Was it such a high
To brag
Look, I killed this stag?

The same stag we heard roar
For a week, maybe more
In the dark of the night –
Can you imagine the sight?
Standing high on the moor, the moon full and the mist...
But through that mist, that ghostly mist,
The finger on the trigger just couldn't resist.
One last, proud, defiant roar
Then...
No more.

No more rebirth from this virile spirit,
                              Regeneration
                    dead in its tracks.
A son of the Forest, majestic and wild,
With sadness, we'll remember our stag
Long after that forgotten brag.

lines following a hunter's poem – Terry Quinn

turning days on a flat white page
telling tales of the hunt
using the hills and valleys of words
to mist what is really a front

this has nothing to do with the country
it's about the heart of mankind
how the ripping apart of foxes
leads on to a man who is blind

and yes I've been at the killing
felt that call of November rain
but I've seen the terror of hunting
as dogs snap into a vein

now England knows of the cruelty
that linked the call of your wild
from shrugs at an animal's suffering
to the blooding of a child

Bird – Liz Berry

When I became a bird, Lord, nothing could not stop me.

     The air feathered
           as I knelt
by my open window for the charm –
           black on gold,
        last star of the dawn.

Singing, they came:
          throstles, jenny wrens,
jack squalors swinging their anchors through the clouds.

     My heart beat like a wing.

I shed my nightdress to the drowning arms of the dark,
my shoes to the sun's widening mouth.

     Bared,
  I found my bones hollowing to slender pipes,
     my shoulder blades tufting down.
    I spread   my flight-greedy arms
to watch my fingers jewelling like ten hummingbirds,
my feet callousing to knuckly claws.
     As my lips calcified to a hooked kiss

silence

     then an exultation of larks filled the clouds
and, in my mother's voice, chorused:
  Tek flight, chick, goo far fer the Winter.

So I left girlhood behind me like a blue egg

                              and stepped off
                    from the window ledge.

How light I was

as they lifted me up from Wren's Nest
bore me over the edgelands of concrete and coal.

I saw my grandmother waving up from her fode,
                    looped
         the infant school and factory,
                    let the zephrs carry me   out to the coast.

Lunars I flew

                    battered and tuneless

         the storms turned me inside out like a fury,
there wasn't one small part of my body didn't bawl.

Until I felt it at last   the rush of squall thrilling my wing
                    and I knew my voice
was no longer words but song   black upon black.

I raised my throat to the wind
                    and this is what I sang . . .

charm birdsong or dawn chorus; *jack squalor* swallow; *fode* yard
From *Black Country* by Liz Berry published by Chatto & Windus.
Reproduced by permission of The Random House Group Ltd. © 2014

The gift – Ben Ray

Often, after the tide had been good
and when my father had visited the homes
of those who could not afford to pay
I would lie awake into the dying evening
my eyes pressed tight shut, as if in prayer –
waiting for the gentle doctors' hand on my shoulder,
before pretending to yawn and stretch from sleep
as he led me outside to the lemon tree by the gate.
They would be hung in plastic bags, shapes throwing
crazy silhouettes onto the lawn in a moonlit puppet show,
or tied by tails on low branches – a surreal fruit
shells shining in rusted red, claws bumping softly together
like windchimes in the soft Mediterranean night.
And only the waving poplars saw us, but promised not to tell
each time as we reeled in our catch, laying them carefully
onto the Renault 4CV's old unsprung back seats
our fingers coarse from rough string and dry saltwater.
I'd watch as their antenna twitched and flicked with life.
No one on the island but us knew of their unnatural migration
back to the ocean, slipping along moonlit roads until –
at last! – my father would haul them out onto the sand
and he would let me pick them up, one by one
hold them under the breakers long enough to wake up
and then slowly letting them wriggle free, passing them back
to the sea

Fallen: to the forest – Dawn Bauling

Hesitant through the pine
trees this morning labouring
slower than canine
cursing the cropped
nature of this wood
weft leeched
into us slyly
stayed by their roots
their ancient verticals.
Every second it takes
to cut, to kill them
is personal.
Our like-loved sap
rises
anticipating November's
inevitable bereavement
loss too queer
to find adequate counsel.
Slow shuttered
we keep them
inner-eyed
as imprints
to peel away
later like slides
once enjoyed
on Sunday afternoons.

Spotted Deer – Pascale Petit

To be spotlit
like a doe
in the forest
at dawn

I would risk
all the leopards
and tigers
even my father's gun

To be spotlit
like a bride
on the aisle
of this cathedral

I would wear
a deer dress
of stars, my legs
light as sunrays

Isn't death sparks
of holy fire?
Better to have heard
the leaves praying

once as the sun
was rising
than remained
safe in the dark

Suicide Hill – Karen Jane Cannon

The retired coalminer came to our cottage,
eyes dark pits, told us
about the sparrowhawks shot on the moor,
protected eggs smashed in the nest.

We knew about the gamekeepers, saw them
each night, sitting in lay-bys
with shotguns, flashlights, waiting
for life to scuttle past—arctic hares caught

between seasons, pale-scut rabbits
eyes round moons, a wildcat stalking shadows—
these moors old breeding grounds
for flame-feathered grouse,

yet the Southern Upland Way beckons,
opening secret passages between hills
for us to lay first treads.
It is suicide to come here—

to lay rare eggs in nests of clanging heather bells.
They know this at the unconsecrated burial ground
at the foot of Green Lowther—suicides
brought from the valley on carts

to lie staring at swirling skies.
But this is where they come to live and die,
to hills as bare as eggs, crowning
the top of the world.

First published in *Mslexia*

Kerfuffle – Alison Brackenbury

Something is in our shed.
The cats stream down the path with eyes like moons.

Something leaps past the barrow, filled with logs.
It blurs a clouded tail.

Something, when I pull you there to look,
lifts two wide ears, triangular.

Old fox, asleep in shed. Do you
dream of nothing?

Published in 'Stand'

Midnight Cull – Kayleigh Campbell

Silence settles on the treetops,
light rain brushes leaves.

Twilight emerges, smiling.
The woodland residents peek out,

enchanted by evening light.
Peaceful sound echoes; birdsong,

fluttering of wing, raindrops.
The sky darkens, wind livens.

A seasoned forest-dweller -
black, white, wiry fur –

scouts snout-first through undergrowth,
foraging a worm for tea.

A step too far -
iron jaws clamp on back legs.

Hopeless struggles and scurrying,
leaves rustling, frantic.

Deep voices, footsteps, torches.
Dogs growling, sniffing, barking.

A rippling gunshot, then   silence.

Brock says – Angela France

delve deep
      under stone
claw sharpstrike into roots
            and earth
find allworld below
      for shelterness

my jaws make a hallowing
of sinless worm and slug

I am needful of night-swart
uncleft in my woodside ledemark

leave sun-tide
      to aquern and wort-cropper
          beingless to me

From *The Hill,* Nine Arches Press, 2017; reprinted by kind permission of the publisher

Elephants – Lauren Mason

Lean closer, inhale – dung, iron. Run your fingers along the braille of her hide, translate its weathering. Read the rot in her flank, clots where her tusks should have been. Find yourself thinking of idols, piano keys. A man like you with a knife, a family. To her side stands a calf, milk-breath fading. All the spells he knows, incanted and failed. His three-day vigil has cast a mandala in widening circles around his mother. The air vibrates – is that a plea caught in a throat; or the wind, insinuating its way in? Step forwards, and he staggers towards you. Step back, and he does not – is left trapped in this lotus of dust and bones. Steady yourself, tread slowly now, hands open and unarmed.

Stopping on Rannoch Moor – Jenny Hamlett

Red deer, two does, several fawns running
from the rap, rap of our footsteps on the road.

Gentle, silent they slip into a cluster of rocks
and scrub without disturbing a leaf.

They stop.

Large ears poke up above the greenery
brown ears edged with white, cuddly like soft toys.

Why don't they move?

Wary, the deep pools of their dark eyes
consider our plodding. Ears flick towards us.

Why wait?

The freedom of the whole of Rannoch Moor
lies ahead. Escape would be easy.

We walk on, round a rocky outcrop,
almost fall over a party of tourists learning to kill.

They are preparing their guns to aim
at a huge, cut-out, wooden stag.

The deer know, stay hidden and safe.
We, the lesser evils, hurry past

the hunters' enthusiasm, as the first report
rips open, a clean, clear sky.

Peace Crane – Denni Turp

I will write peace on your wings and you will fly all over the world.

Sadako Sasaki

Red-crowned cranes bob their splash
of colour in the monochrome landscape
of the Japanese winter on Hokkaido island
in the snow.

They follow every mirrored prancing step
in synchrony, black legs elegantly dancing,
long black necks curling fluid sibilance
with every bow.

Forever is the theme that fills their ballet,
every jump and wingspread black and white
an echo of their voices taking turns to call,
to know

the other sure and certain in the turn and float.
Close on the magic thousand gather here,
breath misting upward from their skyward bills.
Stately, slow,

they stand to still their dance and fold their wings,
while far away across the world, Excel is busy
with the arms fair in full flow,

and pink paper cranes hang on strings to fill the quiet air
in the restaurant below.

Deer – Chrys Salt

Somehow he had leaped the cattle-grid
to meet us head-on in the lane.
We stood stock still to hide
willing him back the way he came,
or, thinking us trees or rocky outcrops, pass.

Caught between cattle-grid, a gate
and us, his tiptoe ballerina hooves
zigzagged for egress from the stony place, his great
glass- marble eyes refracting beech-leaf, foxglove,
the fragile featherheads of meadow-grass.

We were so close to him we smelled his fright,
wanted his escape, but felt the privilege
of him too great to move and light
the touch-paper of panic. So we lay siege
with stillness, marvelling at his beauty and his grace.

Minutes must have passed before
he knew his enemy for what we were
and terror projected him through light and air
across the grid again, to vanish in a gloom of fir
the bloodstain of the sun on rock and gorse.

Deer by Loch Tay – Seth Crook

None in the day.
They come down in darkness,
stay until dawn.

With the nibbled kale,
the gnawed turnips,
you'd be baffled.

Unless you stepped out
carrying a lamp,
saw your fields full

of the quiet vagrants
whose lives are distant,
however close they are.

If they culled us,
they'd have every right;
hanging us up in bits,

in freezers,
in sheds,
stomping on all lamps.

Let there be light, we say,
Let there be darkness,
they answer, racing for their hills.

Zoological Society of London – Martyn Crucefix

Today they weigh all the inmates of the zoo
they must lure them onto scales
with fish or fruit or seeds or scraps of meat
because they are not happy to be so coerced
to squat or stand or slump on their sides
while the telling needles quiver to a stop
to still all this rebelliousness of life
see the penguins will not peaceably queue
and antelopes shy and shiver out of line
pawing the dirt of their enclosures
as parrots tip defiant heads already heavily-armed
with nut-cracking bills they sense
a fight in the offing and indeed from all sides
there's a shriek a growl a roar
though if you ask the green-jacketed keepers
they're sure it's done for the animals' good
but the pygmy hippo remains unconvinced
and drowns herself deeper the flamingos hide
under pink wings and the guys in green
have no sweet voice or lyre
so camels continue to peel back their jagger lips
to show filthy teeth the big cats hunker down
and glare sidelong from their superiority
but it seems the bald-headed eagle cannot resist
the eviscerated rat left to ooze on the scales
and by lunchtime half the penguins have been freed
back into their pool's oily glint
and progress has been made on the colobus monkeys
but slowly being so difficult to catch
and the monitor lizard
can only really be *invited* to come forward

to stroll across the waiting scales
the black bear thankfully is sleepy enough
in her improvised sling and perhaps
she hardly knows what's happening to her
and it's not clear if great shoals of fins
are reduced to kilos or whether clouds of wings
are assessed in their thousands
to be converted to individuals
by some pre-set programme or smart algorithm
but it fascinates that so much blood scale flesh
horn and bone should eventually
come chattering from banks of printers
till finally the day's exhausted twilight falls
and a breeze blows sheets of newsprint
slowly past the gorillas' empty cages
the headlines lost—then seen—then lost again
in a spooling litany into the distance
and here's a glimpse of a story from the Gale Crater
on the Martian planet's surface
where the probe 'Curiosity' is still weighing dust

Find A Place To Lie – Mike McNamara

Find a place for me to lie
between the suckling vixen
and the slumbering vole.
Soft and warm
within the belly of this dark clay.
Anoint my face
with the blood of the mistletoe
and know
that I shall not be woken
by the sound of stones that roll away

Buddha Garden, Gardoussel – Roselle Angwin

I won't say that even in paradise
there is a snake
but I will say that even in this garden
death too has its dwelling-place –
the butterfly knocked by careless feet
whose wings can no longer bear its weight
the plump vole in the tortoiseshell cat's teeth
the little and greater losses we admit to
in each of our own life's orbit –

Last night in the perfect wooded hills
against a perfect twilit sky
la chasse began, and the shots
seemed to ricochet off every tree
until the whole great bowl
of the valley fractured and cracked
could no longer hold

And below something in me broke too
at another absence at a human hand
another tear in the weave of things –
the rip now that had been a deer, and again a deer
and a boar – great savage chasms
opening at the edges of this our more-than-human family
and into which each of us also must fall.

A Guided Tour – Kabul – Frances Sackett

'The lion is blind
His pelt in ragged tufts.
He is the last inhabitant of our zoo.

'He used to have a name.
So did the other animals and birds.
Now they have been stolen for food
And he is just LION.'

We tour past twisted bars
And broken cages,
Glimpse the ruined garden.

'When the hand grenade
Blew up his face
The city doctors battled for his sight.

'He is our symbol now,
Our hope of regaining dignity;
Regaining our own front doors.

'This was my house.
Here on this very street.
If I step on the pavement
I'll be broken like lion.

'You see the wall I built,
It hides my door.
It hides my blossom tree.

'You see the snow,
Lighting up the mountains,
The blossom comes like that.'

Published in *STAPLE* 1997 & *Sing for the Inner Ear* – Sandburg,
Livesay Anthology

Imagine – Shanta Acharya

The song of humpbacked whales,
breath of life flowing through conch shells,

uniquely decorated flukes falling on waves,
huge white flippers slapping the water.

Imagine a grizzly bear on its haunches
in the bend of the river scooping up silver slivers,
tossing minnows into its yawning mouth.

Forests, canyons, rivers, waterfalls, double rainbows,
the laughter of lightning holding us in thrall.

Blush of a bride, the sky at sunrise, sunset,
spreading in wild abandonment.

Imagine cloud formations of changing configurations,
dove white to crow black, altocumulus to tornado chasers.

Smile of a camel filling the loneliness of a desert,
a cheetah in motion, the dance of King Cobras.

Sighing of leaves when the wind gives them a shake,
hawks soaring on tides of air, wild wings streamlined.

A colony of bats singing, meditating upside down
on an ancient tree grown large as a grandparent.

The majesty of a reclusive snow leopard disappearing
in a blizzard on the slopes of Mount Everest.

A smoking volcano blowing spectacular hoops
of fire, pouring molten lava for days,
depositing ash on the tray of land.

Imagine a stately cavalcade of moving mountains of ice
in the Arctic, shimmering with the aurora borealis.

Brightly coloured wings of a butterfly hovering,
their translucency in moonlight revealing...

Now open your eyes wide and imagine
our rich world bereft of nature's blessing.

Shanta Acharya, *Imagine: New and Selected Poems* (HarperCollins, India, 2017)

Sleeping Black Jaguar – Pascale Petit

1

A solar eclipse – his fur
seems to veil light,
the smoulder

of black rosettes
a zoo of sub-atoms
I try to tame –

tritium, lepton, anti-proton.
They collide
as if smashed inside

a particle accelerator.
But it's just Aramis sleeping,
twitching himself back

to the jungle, where he leaps
into the pool of a spiral
galaxy, to catch a fish.

2

Later, the keeper tells me
Aramis has had surgery
for swallowing

a hose-head
where his hank of beef
was lodged. But

what vet could take
a scalpel to this
dreaming universe?

What hand could shave
that pelt, to probe
the organs

of dark matter, untwist
time's intestines
and stitch

night's belly
together again, only
to return him to a cage?

From *Fauverie*, Seren, 2014; reprinted by kind permission of the publisher.

Fox – Angela France

      is my namen
            man slurs me elles
      clithe not to my ruddy hide
my ledemark tithing is all
   the dun I tread
            coneys and wort-croppers
are underyoke to me
   bow to my holyroom
         under delvern and root

niht-time is mine   evenleether
with brock and nadder
      leafworm and wanderlight
my wif is a bale-fire at swart-time
   calling wellstemned

I wend where I will
         seave and rede
            fox is my namen

From *The Hill,* Nine Arches Press, 2017; reprinted by kind permission
of the publisher

Hognap – Maggie Mackay

I'm a gobbler of slugs,
beetles, caterpillars, snails,
a digger, a climber, a swimmer.
dusk heralds my 'to do' time,
spring, summer, autumn.

By Halloween I'm a fat forager
for leaves in suburban gardens,
wilted countryside bracken,
reeds by a bittern's hiding ground.
I'm a busy builder in a hidden pocket,
maybe a hedgerow, tree root,
under logs, under sheds.

Locate my hibernaculum, if you can,
insulated, watertight, fit for winter torpor,
a refuge for my heartbeat of twenty per minute.

Do not disturb.

The Badger – John Clare

When midnight comes a host of dogs and men
Go out and track the badger to his den,
And put a sack within the hole and lie
Till the old grunting badger passes by.
He comes and hears - they let the strongest loose.
The old fox hears the noise and drops the goose.
The poacher shoots and hurries from the cry,
And the old hare half wounded buzzes by.
They get a forkéd stick to bear him down
And clap the dogs and take him to the town,
And bait him all the day with many dogs,
And laugh and shout and fright the scampering hogs.
He runs along and bites at all he meets:
They shout and hollo down the noisy streets.
He turns about to face the loud uproar
And drives the rebels to their very door.
The frequent stone is hurled wher'er they go;
When badgers fight, then everyone's a foe.
The dogs are clapped and urged to join the fray;
The badger turns and drives them all away.
Though scarcely half as big, demure and small,
He fights with dogs for hours and beats them all.
The heavy mastiff, savage in the fray,
Lies down and licks his feet and turns away.
The bulldog knows his match and waxes cold
The badger grins and never leaves his hold.
He drives the crowd and follows at their heels
And bites them through - the drunkard swears and reels.
The frighted women take the boys away,
The blackguard laughs and hurries on the fray.
He tries to reach the woods, an awkward race,

But sticks and cudgels quickly stop the chase.
He turns again and drives the noisy crowd
And beats the many dogs in noises loud.
He drives away and beats them every one,
And then they loose them all and set them on.
He falls as dead and kicked by boys and men,
Then starts and grins and drives the crowd again;
Till kicked and torn and beaten out he lies
And leaves his hold and cackles, groans and dies.

The Sea Singers – Verity Schanche

A freak show
my sonar broken
I try to navigate this alien water
its obstructions and noises,
tight edges and eye-piercing lights.
My drowned memories slowly surface.
We were called the sea singers, sea guardians
travelling the whale's road
our voyages charted in songs
our calves beside us, sewing
through the sea like silk
as they learnt their pathways
through the world's oceans.
We were peaceful in our pristine kingdom.

A Captive Large Pacific Striped Octopus Pities Humans – Simon Williams

The whitecoats try to hide against the walls,
but their heads and extremities give them away.
I can see through the glass, when they leave,
they change colour again, bright as clown fish.

They're all so backboned, stiff as coral,
can't squeeze into a crevice to frustrate a conger.
They take pride in angles, put straight entrances on everything,
try as they will to move without contact. They jabber.

The real pity is their poor arms,
only two really, only five pads on each.
How can they touch with those; no suction,
even underwater, and claws like beaks to clack?

They have no skills with suckers, no way to pull or release.
They can't embrace with those boned limbs.
How do they calm an angry one or slip
a spermatophore into a fluttering syphon?

The Terrier Men – Jaine Wild

It is of nasty deeds they work
The undercover men who lurk
Amongst the bracken of the woods,
And heed and humble of the hunt –
They work throughout with dog and spade
While leafy coverts hide and shade
The cruelness of those men…

Who wait without a conscience past?
And watch the fox run very fast
For hounds are at its very heel
And so for safety home it goes –
Amid the blood-curdling throes
Of foxhound calls and huntsmen's whips...

So hence they come those men with spades and fork,
And terrier dogs that pull on their leads
Followed by huntsmen with bloodthirsty needs.
Whips that crack, wind that calls
Branches breaking, in the fall
Of life's torment to our wild creatures…

Dogs pull forth, from the very hole of the earth
A panic-stricken fox,
Teeth that gnash and bite the throat
Blood that pours onto the shiny coat
Of a small pregnant frightened being.
Huntsmen smile, terrier men cheer
Their callous ways have left them without seeing,
A cruel and barbaric trade,
Dug with blood spattered fork and spade.
Red coated within the word tradition…

Then finally when they have had their play
Off they go – the end of day.
And what is left is covered in dirt.
A tiny sliver of bloody liver
An intestinal trail that was part of your frail
Body, ripped alive by hungry dogs trained in 'sport' –
Its screams that echoed in your wood
Where those sadists had recently stood.

Chiddingfold, Leconfield Hunt, end of a dig out

Seal Sister Song – Philip Gross
for Selkie

boat   drifts
waves heave and lift
and nothing is still in their rise and fall
except.... something slight
in the dazzle of light
a long way out and very small
but what   but who
could be waiting for you
her smooth head cocked as if listening to
the song that the sea wind sings ?

beneath the surf's roar
and the hiss of the spray
listen...   and go on listening
as you stand on the shore
at the edge of the day
and they say she will come if you sing

quiet   wise
those patient eyes
tell me, sister, what do you know?
sunset   sunrise
and the ebb of tides
I know that the people drift by on their flow
that children born
and children grown
return with children of their own
and this is the song the sea sings

```
        night          sleep
        on the face of the deep
  and the moon on the dark sea   glistening
        sister seal
        swims into your dream
  *and you'll come, yes, you'll come when she sings*
        *when she sings: Sister, remember me*
  *and you'll come, yes, you'll come when she sings*
```

Hooked kiss – Miriam Calleja

Inspired by Liz Berry's poem *Bird*

I could not control
         my joints
     how does this work?
         how do I get comfortable?
would I ever? And
would I ever enjoy my bird-ness?

They taught me how:
           the others, using air
using wind, to help, be in the flow, be in tune

I didn't need you, lord
     I needed my eyes and my instinct

           Bold,
my purpose, my ambitions changed,
I was part of something new
     I spread myself as part of the universal
essence, beauty was easy to me, natural
     I tiptoed around in this knowledge
         I was magical and needed
to sing

In Holm Wood – Jean Atkin

Galloway

The Minnoch dapples, fly-danced.
At noon we find a shiver on the water
suggesting stars at midnight.

Soaking wet bracken and grasses muffle
this September wood. Thin pink heather
and purple scabious light it.

Here are vast stones that stopper a dyke-end
where a dead thorn tree stands
like its own ghost, blurred with moss.

We walk and lichen flowers
on every fallen branch and acorns split
and green at every step.

We breathe in oak-air, laced
with draughts of peat and the sudden
swing of a jay.

Not Lost Since Last Time, from Oversteps Books in 2013

At a Distance – Meg Gannon

It seems so remote
so easy at a distance,
simply to call it a sport,
to raise a hand, a gun.

But get close, see
that liquid eye, its light
become dull in death,
feel a body, still warm,
but bloody.

There is no triumph
in taking life so vital,
destroying a creature that,
moments before, lifted its head
to take in the cool air.

The Thought-Fox – Ted Hughes

I imagine this midnight moment's forest:
Something else is alive
Besides the clock's loneliness
And this blank page where my fingers move.
Through the window I see no star:
Something more near
Though deeper within darkness
Is entering the loneliness:

Cold, delicately as the dark snow,
A fox's nose touches twig, leaf;
Two eyes serve a movement, that now
And again now, and now, and now

Sets neat prints into the snow
Between trees, and warily a lame
Shadow lags by stump and in hollow
Of a body that is bold to come

Across clearings, an eye,
A widening deepening greenness,
Brilliantly, concentratedly,
Coming about its own business

Till, with sudden sharp hot stink of fox
It enters the dark hole of the head.
The window is starless still; the clock ticks,
The page is printed.

From *The Hawk in the Rain* 1957 Reprinted with permission Faber and Faber

Badger – Jackie Biggs

He looks at her without seeing;
her breath catches at his beauty
as she watches.

His secrets are hidden in darkness
dusk-time creature rummaging and rooting,
heavy and strong, yet he glides
lightfooted over the earth

goes about his business in private
touches no-one,
is confident, solid, secure,
self-contained in his honest life.

Nose-twitching head lifts,
ears prick, a stick cracks …
he's off, the stocky swagger
powers forward,   disappears.

He knows only his dark world.
he lives in the underground,
has no need of us.

Yet he is significant to us,
so that we can blame him

reproach him for our shortcomings
and seek to damage him, blamelessly,
simply because he lives.

But they shall not have him now.
He is free to breathe his noble and gracious air
as he travels lightfooted through his world.
And his earth will claim him in its own time.

First published in *The Spaces in Between* Pinewood Press, Swansea, 2015

Bait Dog – Rosemary McLeish

I stopped following a friend on Facebook
because one morning she posted a picture
of a bait dog, I think it was after a fight.
Trussed in a roundish ball,
no sign of limbs or tail,
its face had more stitches than flesh.
It (far beyond being a he or she) looked like
a lump of meat with eyes.
Every stitch reflected in their suffering.
My fellow humans did this to a dog

I was ill at the time.
I didn't want to see this.
I don't want such images appearing
on my Newsfeed over breakfast.

I couldn't get it out of my head.
It made me physically sick.
When I lay down at night
it played over and over like an earworm.
It felt like it became part of my flesh
a hallucinated image from drugs
or schizophrenia.

A hole in the hare's ear where a shot went through – Lynn Woollacott

Jack speeds through the oaks, down the bank,
dives under pond lilies, emerges on the other side
into the bloodied floating weed where two drakes fell dead.

He streams across the far side of the pond
with dog-paddle paws, a frown of brown fur,
cold water on his belly, whiskers on the water.

A magpie flies across with alarm chatter,
water-boatmen frantically circle on the water,
Jack aim for the straightest line.

There's loud baying from the woods.
The air is tinged with the scent of blood, shot
and stagnant water. Jack reaches the opposite bank.

Ears upright, no backtracking, he's leaping
down the feed stream. Surely in the clear?
Black leeches wind across to the blood lines.

Men and dogs arrive. Dogs whine by the water,
one prey gone, another for the taking?
The men lower their guns and stand hands on hips.

Seahorse – Kathy Miles

Corralled in its box,
a childhood's guilty treasure.
I loved his papery rustle, the tail
that curved my finger, the spiny head
with its coronet. I wanted to take him
down to the shore, float him on the waves,
see him wake as his body filled with water
and he swam to join his herd.
A slow dressage between the reeds,
his neck bridled by seagrass
as he rode the long gyres home.

Beyond Broadwoodwidger – Marc Woodward

Let us suppose your car packs up
out here. Beyond Broadwoodwidger,
St Giles On The Heath, Virginstow.
It is night — a justice of darkness
that lives on these shapeless acres.
You walk the twisted lane a mile
then, seeing lights, you cut across.
Fields, hedges, a dark-shadowed copse.
Fields, gates, the woodland edge.
What do you feel?
The brief breath of an owl;
the waiting silence after the fox's cough.
What do you hear?
The weight of condensation
on an ocean of bending blades.
A hundred rabbits knew your sound
through the earth, long before the air
announced your voice or waved your scent.
Here there is nothing to save you.
If you lie down now this wet ditch
may be your decomposing place.
Who will find you? Only strangers.
Still the darkness will keep moving,
eating, weather-bound, star-stared.
Out here, in the twitch of spiders,
the fright of jays, the quick knee-jerk
of a cricket's ear — a moment
considered, passing, forgotten.
The only trace: a disturbance
in the scent blown down from the wood;
an imprint on the retina of a cow's large soft eye, fading.

Badger – Emma-Jane Hughes

Stupid dual carriageway traffic.

Crane neck to quell children's quarrel.
Creep forward – glimpse something
half up the grassy bank, stretched.
Direct children to sign on the other side.

Huge badger – must be a brock.
Motionless, in daylight.
Quell urge to climb bank,
curl around broad back.

The Otter's Holt – Barbara E Robinson

(R.I.P. John, our River Bailiff)

I spied the otters as they taught their young,
to swim, to feed as it was meant to be,
it was a favourite childhood memory,
sweet Nature's gift to cherish, to be sung.

When they left their riverside holt that day
those gleaming creatures oh so wary, shy....
Entranced I watched them diving, swimming by,
unknowing that their future spelt affray.

But soon the wicked ways of man were wrought,
within each stream and river of this land...
Most otters culled as deadly contraband,
and we true country folk left most distraught.

They came, they saw and took each otter's life,
no soul, compassion for those creatures fine,
now named as thieves of every fishing line
Nature's ways soon involved in bitter strife.

No reason can condone that deathly cull,
nor call it sport mankind can glory in.
Demeaning nature was man's greatest sin,
for their own benefit, their senses dulled.

Understorey – Deborah Harvey

Your father in his fawn windcheater
names the song of each bird we hear
points out fox holes and fungi,
pulls to one side an elder branch
explains how those dollops of blossom
became this darkening fruit.

As he lets go the branch swings back
like the beams of cranes overhead
building conference halls, brand new departments
or the CCTV in these MOD car parks
that monitor visitors, trespassers,
swivelling on their plinths.

Splatts Wood presses up against its fence
like a rescue dog without a home,
it has a Committee of Friends, a down-
loadable Management Plan.
A survey of birds takes place in the spring,
the ride on its southern edge is a bats' commuter route.

One night as I'm walking to my car
I hear a roe deer
plunging through its understorey
and the next time I happen to see your father
the skin of his arms is elderberry purple,
his face is a cliff.

Taken in flight – M.R. Hume

Through damp mist, wings fly,
red, green, gold, flash in dawn's light;
gundogs wait their call.

Game – M.R. Hume

We breed them; kill them.
Their life means nothing; their worth?
The act of killing

Prey – Chrissy Banks

I have been a deer in dreams.
I have been a fox.

I have run for my life as I slept,
the hunt at my back.

I have felt my lungs ache,
my heart pummelling my chest,

so close they were
I could smell their sweat.

I've choked on silence as I opened
my mouth to shout for help.

There was a pack at my heels
who would rip me apart.

I didn't know why.
Nor does the fox or the deer.

On a small hill seeded with stone – K. V. Skene

fresh scat, thistle, cock's foot, sedge and the sloughed skin of an
adder we almost overlook the thin scratchings of bunting and
finch as they fling themselves into the spitting teeth of an east
wind, instinctively challenging the unseasonable worrying above,
something nobody ever is totally prepared for while, shoulders
hunched, hands thrust into pockets we learn we are no longer who
we were although it's only our habit of walking out in all kinds
that shaped these old boots on our feet as well as the greedy
ground-swell of hummocks and waterlogged ditches which web
these footpaths and bridleways however this has become so
habitual we never talk about it nor the changeable weather nor the
time it now takes us to step out of ordnance survey 164 and stop,
look and listen as memory unzips its anorak and an out-of-sight
train slams through the distant early morning as this ordinary day
struggles to its feet, a new-born lamb, and stares up as if it
remembers us being here before, behind different faces perhaps
and there a red kite circles and here's the slight imprint of deer-
slots under the apple tree, its blossoms splashing and we drown,
our eyes rinsed clear as spring water.

Previously Published: *Orbis*, 146, Winter 2009 (UK)

I am That Salmon – Raine Geoghegan

She dives deep
into crisp cold waters,
splices through changing currents,
springs up towards the sun
then down into
welcoming watery arms.
Above her, a fish,
or something foreign
shimmying in the light.
A split second and she is there,
opening her mouth in anticipation,
closing it on a sharp sly hook.
Spawn like bubbles pop around her.
Flashes of blue, green, yellow
fade into grey.
Pulled out of the river,
she is thrown onto an alien bed.
It is dry, coarse.
She lies choking, quivering,
ripples of water spill onto the bank,
never to reach her.

*'I am that salmon as the hook is taken out of her mouth
and I watch the light in her eyes slowly fade.'*

Field 'Sport' – Vivien Foulkes-James

Through the trees comes a chilling sound,
yelping hounds, menacing hooves,
in a split second he turns and takes fright.

Terrified he runs for cover
desperation drives him on.
Through the wood, the field yet further
sure-footed, brilliant, he flashes by.
The blood lust call is louder, louder,
hooves on hard earth, closing in.
Confusion rules, his movements falter,
weary, tired, he must go on.

Too late
the 'game' is up,
his escape route blocked.
To the shrieks of humans,
his perfect body is torn apart.

Deer Field – Maggie Smith

My daughter wants to know where the deer are.
We used to see them across the street
from the airports long-term parking lots,
before backhoes tore down the trees
and piled them in the grass. At the intersection
of Broad and James, I tell her all of this
was forest before we were born, and it was
full of deer, but they had to leave
when people cleared the land for buildings—
 that gas station, that drug store—and roads,
like the one we're on now. She says
it makes her sad. The few bare trees left
are leafed with black birds, wings trembling
a little in the wind. The sky is a single sheet
of corrugated cloud—rippled but seamless
as if to prove it was not manufactured.
She doesn't ask what they are building
by the airport, in what we called Deer Field.
It doesn't matter. I have changed her.
I have given her the first in a long list
of disappointments, clearing away
a perfect, wild space in her to make room.

'Deer Field' from *Good Bones*, published by Tupelo Press, copyright
2017 Maggie Smith. Used with permission

First Hunt – Belinda Rimmer

A boy in camouflage and tracking boots
heads into a forest. Ducks and grouse forgotten,
as well they might be, in this the season of deer.

His father, who teaches him hunting ways,
tiptoes and skitters, sips whisky from a hip flask.
They stop at the watering place.

A soft-skinned stag jumps from the trees,
lifts his antlered head, breathes
and scents the damp air.

Between the boy's fingers is cold metal.
He kneels. Doesn't meet the stag's eyes.
Takes aim.   His first kill.

Beyond the slaughtered animal the sun rises.
A fine day but the boy sees darkness,
like pages of black crayon or fairytale devils.

A strange new feeling lodges in his chest.
He wants the stag to stand, bold and beloved,
to be nothing but the bringer of morning.

Dear Rhino – Angela Topping

I'm sorry
for ever thinking
your horn
your magnificent curving horn
made of keratin
could be any use
to cure humans
of fevers,
or make them better.
I was wrong.

I'm sorry too
for all the horns
mounted on
wooden shields
as trophies.
No-one these days
can bear the sight
much less
want to put them
up on walls
for all to see.
Not even museums.

How could I
have thought
your magnificent curving horn
would look good
anywhere except on you,
you great wardrobe
of a vegetarian
water-hole drinker?

I'm sorry I ever
started this
now you are growing scarce.
Can you ever forgive me?

A Buzzard Moment – Gareth Culshaw

Then my eyes were caught,
like a book falling from
a shelf, a buzzard happened.

Her wings gave the air
a life, a breath, a reason.

She took the fields
and made them wave
under her body.

She played with the sunlight
before gliding past the trees

entering the wood
            like a foot in a boot.

I turned away happy.

Only to be thrown grave

by the sound of gunshots.

Our brief encounter with dragons and damsels – Jan Harris

Southern Hawkers dart forwards
to inspect us, pinning themselves
to the world's fabric

like Fabergé brooches.
Jewelled and enamelled in green and blue
they razzle-dazzle us, speed away.

We step to the water's edge, where bulrushes
wear the mysterious skins of nymphs -
reminders of life before surface glamour.

Earlier, we saw fossils under glass,
the delicate tracery of veins -
a primeval language phrased in rock,

translated here by the Downy Emerald
in flight, the panes of her wings
slick as bubble mixture on a wand.

A Beautiful Demoiselle settles on my hand,
wings folded like the pages of a manuscript
illuminated with ultramarine.

We are figures sketched in the margins,
dots on his timeline,
our heads turned as he disappears.

Girl and Hare – Sasha Dugdale

There was once a girl and she had a hare
as a pet. It was so long and brown and soft.
It stretched its body next to hers on the sunlounger
where she lay in her oversized sunglasses,
little and freckled. The hare had the tautness of game
its hindquarters were round and solid
but she could nest its paws in her hand
ring them with her fingers as a poacher might, but tenderly.
When the sun was bright she could see through the hare's hindlegs,
its thin skin, thrown hurriedly over bone and tendon,
the light pulsed red and sombre as if the hare itself contained
a small convex sun like a red blood cell.
Hare had a narrow breast like hers, rosed with fur, and little childish
      shoulders
but forearms like a strong man's, the sinews and fibres twanging
      soundlessly as it shifted.
Now it lay still, although hares never sleep, its lip moving gently and
      its amber eyes waxing and waning.
It lowered its lids, for a moment it looked sly, knowing.
Hare is apparently drowsing. The girl removes her glasses, places
      them on hare's face
and closes her eyes.
This is hare's moment: as long as her, and as old.

Of things we cannot know – Dawn Bauling
(at Gentle Jane)

After another wet day
we take to the beach
for a late trickle of   sun

Down the slate track
from our borrowed home,
past the gypsy caravan,   beyond.

He's cracking slate, s k i m m ing
between ball-bouncing
for a dog that's loved twice.

His patience peels us both,
making hard layers
become known, soft,   opened.

He smiles,   above me,
talking of the dozen swans
he's seen again   and heard.

They are singing of things
we cannot know he says.
Perhaps   in the shift   we can.

Vixen Eclipse – Lesley Quayle

Vixen snaked through the pines as earth slipped into twilight and a black moon rode bare back over the pagan sun. Her copper pelt blazed like wildfire, while all around the world drowsed in untimely dusk.

The moon began to slide from its solar anchorage, unmoored on a cuticle of light and vixen froze, tongue lolling through a jagged chine of white teeth. Time stilled. The moon tiptoed back to its lunar edge-land.

Vixen ran, flaring through the barley stubble like a beacon.

Everyone Sang – Siegfried Sassoon

Everyone suddenly burst out singing;
And I was filled with such delight
As prisoned birds must find in freedom,
Winging wildly across the white
Orchards and dark-green fields; on - on - and out of sight.

Everyone's voice was suddenly lifted;
And beauty came like the setting sun:
My heart was shaken with tears; and horror
Drifted away ... O, but Everyone
Was a bird; and the song was wordless; the singing will never be done.

Deer Folklore – Amelia Starling

Faerie Cattle, Sacred, Sika, and Our Wild Sides

I feel a close affinity with deer. They can be timid creatures, and this lends them an almost mythical reputation in some places. The elusive deer, somewhere in the woods, quiet and unseen. Maybe watching you. No harm in that. Just watching, and then slipping away. Yet underneath that timidness they hold wisdom, and strength. They know their terrain, and when danger is near, and how to protect themselves.

Deer feature in the folklore of many countries. From my travels, I have come across them in Scotland and Japan. Their stories form a link between our world and the animal kingdom, and affect how we interact with these genteel creatures.

Deer in Scotland

Many Scottish legends associate deer with faeries. For one thing, deer already possess fae-like qualities. Their bodies are lean and their movements graceful, and they prefer to be hidden from human eyes. Yet they tolerate the presence of faeries. In the Highlands, red deer are said to be the faeries' cattle, providing them with milk. In turn, the faeries protect them by targeting hunters with enchanted arrows. To be hit with a faerie arrow is fateful indeed. You'll likely get a nasty dose of elf-shot, which can be cured by a healer if you're lucky. If you're less lucky, you'll fall down and appear dead to humanity, but your soul will be carried away to Elfhame, the world of the fae.

If a hunter succeeded in killing a deer, the faeries would torment them. There is a story from the Isle of Mull, about a deer hunter called Big Hugh. After killing a deer at Torness, he was carrying it home with his friend who asked him if the deer was heavy. Big Hugh said that it was, and so his friend stuck a penknife in the deer and then asked again. Big Hugh said it felt so much lighter, he could hardly tell that he was carrying it. The extra weight had been put upon him by the faeries, and the penknife counteracted their magic.

Some faerie women also transform themselves into deer, and often encounter hunters whilst in this form. A well-known story from Irish and Scottish mythology tells of Oisín, a great bard of the legendary warriors, the Fianna. His father was Fionn Mac Cumhail, the leader of the Fianna, and his mother was Sadhbh, a woman under a spell which changed her into a deer. Only when in the presence of the Fianna could she regain her human shape. Whilst on a hunting trip, Fionn found Sadhbh and they fell in love. Soon she became pregnant, but their happiness wasn't to last. The magician who had enchanted Sadhbh returned and tricked her into leaving Fionn. Once more a deer, she ran away and gave birth to her baby boy in the forest. He was found many years later by his father, and named Oisín which means 'little deer.'

In Scottish folklore, there is a slightly different version of events. Oisín's mother was a woman called Grainnhe. After being tricked away from Fionn, she was transformed into a white hind and kept under the magician's power. When Fionn found Oisín, he had a patch of deer's hair on his forehead. After Grainnhe's death, her body was released by the magician. The Fianna buried her on the Isle of Skye.

Deer in Japan

In the city of Nara, the old capital of Japan, deer roam free. These are *sika* or spotted deer, which are native to East Asia and have white spots on their backs. At the end of a lantern-lit path, where Nara Park begins to disintegrate into the Kasuga Primeval Forest, stands Kasuga-Taisha. This Shinto shrine is a sacred place for deer, with a deer statue adorning its *temizuya* (purifying water fountain) and a variety of deer *omamori* (charms) for sale. There are four deities enshrined here, one being Takemikazuchi-no-Mikoto, the god of thunder from Kashima in Ibaraki Prefecture. According to Japanese mythology, Takemikazuchi-no-Mikoto came to visit Nara riding upon a white deer. Since then, the deer of Nara were believed to be messengers of the gods. At Kasuga-Taisha you can also purchase white deer figurines with *omikuji* (fortunes). Apart from being adorable, these also hark back to this belief. They are literally holding divine messages about your future in their little porcelain mouths. Choose wisely.

The reputation of Nara deer became so prolific that until the 1600s, harming one was an offence punishable by death. Today they are considered national treasures, and as such are well protected. They are also well fed, since thousands of tourists visit Nara to give them *shika senbei* (deer crackers). The protocol for feeding a Nara deer is first to bow, and then wait for the deer to bow in return before relinquishing the cracker. However, in practice, I just got ganged up on by a group of excited, hungry deer... so unfortunately I cannot vouch for their manners!

Meeting the Nara deer was a profound experience. It was the closest I had ever been to a wild animal, and they were gentle and sweet, but unlike domesticated animals you could simultaneously see their wariness. Their delay before approaching, and how they remained still and poised, as ready to flee at any moment as they were willing to accept my affection. I wanted to reassure them; to make them feel safe. But without their wildness, they wouldn't be the same. And not all humans bare good intentions, so what good would I be doing if I taught them to trust and then the next people they encountered were less compassionate?

I have made many trips to Nara. My friends and colleagues in Japan jestingly nicknamed me '*shika-onna*' (deer lady) because I love them so much. One trip which sticks in my mind is New Year's Eve 2016. It was around 11pm, and dark. I was alone, just behind Todaiji Temple, and I saw a *torii* gate leading into darkness. Everywhere else was lantern lit, except for this path. I took it. I crept up a hill gnarled with tree roots and deer tracks. I could hear them, rustling in the trees on either side of me. When I reached the top, there was a small clearing with a closed shrine (I later learned its name is Tamukeyama-Hachimangu). It was only me, with the trees, the stars, and the hidden deer. In that moment, I felt at home with them. Away from the other humans, out in the forest. I wasn't afraid. The deer were not afraid. I trusted them.

Deer in Fairy Tales

In the Grimms' fairy tale 'Little Brother and Little Sister,' two siblings run away into the forest. The brother drinks from an enchanted stream, and the water transforms him into a deer. His sister cares for him and refuses for them to be separated. Even in death, her spirit returns to check his wellbeing and ultimately break the spell. It's almost as though they are two parts of one being, which simultaneously cannot be complete alone and cannot co-exist as a whole. In his book *The Uses of Enchantment*, Bruno Bettelheim writes that 'they represent the animal and spiritual sides of our personality, which become separated [in the story] but must be integrated for human happiness.' Bettelheim doesn't state which way round he intends the roles to be, leaving readers to make their own decision. The deer can represent the 'animal' part of us; the part which is wild and carefree, whereas the human sister is the seeing and thinking spirit. But these roles could also easily be reversed: The deer can be seen as spiritual for his innocence and closeness to nature, and the sister animalistic for her contentment with living alone in the forest away from other human company.

Deer are often described as guardians of forests, especially stags who are akin to royalty in the woodland animal hierarchy. The brother becoming a deer comes with a certain amount of status. However, whilst the sister grows into a woman, he remains a fawn. As noted by Heidi Anne Heiner in SurLaLune's annotations for the story, 'the sister is the adult figure,' having to arrange food and shelter and make decisions for them both, whilst as a deer the brother is free from responsibility. Eventually the sister becomes a princess, whilst the brother never gets to rut and have the chance to rule the forest. The spell does more than merely change his physical form. It freezes him in time, taking away his progression into adulthood. This story reminds us of the connection to our animal and spiritual sides, and also the need for learning and new experiences to move forward in life.

Deer have much impact on how we view natural spaces, and the stories which come out of them. Whether they truly are messengers of the gods or not, deer are creatures with flesh, blood, and feelings – not just characters from folk tales. That magical, tenuous moment in Nara when they chose to stay beside me reminded me that, for all our stories about wild animals, the only way to understand them is to see them.

Originally published on *The Willow Web*

Badger – Andy Allan

His face is lost in lines of light
cast by swaying hazel shadows.
Motionless, dark legs invisible,
nose-tasting cool air, he bristles
with thrawn determination.
Wary, seeking prey, voles
perhaps, then off again scurrying,
short legs hurrying, head down,
wet grass soaking his belly.
Frogs are on his mind most likely,
always juicy, delicious, acceptable.

Nostrils quiver, sift the breeze.
Abrupt stop. Fox! Somewhere close.
Moon-glow shimmers through
waving reed-rattle.
Focused, he hears movement in
the scrape of grasses by his foot.
The wheel of life turns a little.
Snatching instinctively, jaws crunch
through cartilage and thin bones.
Night stills. He pauses for a moment
then shuffles into moon-shade
and disappears.

They Had No Choice – Phil Knight

is the chosen epitaph
for the vast hecatomb
of animals sacrificed
in Britain's abattoirs of war.

Almost hidden in Hyde Park
in London, the silent stones
of the 'ANIMALS IN WAR memorial
speak for those who had no voice,

that could be understood by
Pressman, General or Politician.
The carvings commemorate the countless
lost lives of dogs, cats, mules, oxen,

donkeys, pigeons and millions of horses.
From the colonial territories camels
and elephants who did their bit for empire.
The poppies do not bloom for them.

Now for these nameless silent ones
only these stones stand in mute eternal
testament of the nobility of beasts
and the bestiality of Man.

Great Crested Newt – Annest Gwilym

In the wood's stippled light
a deadened pond full of mud
and last year's decaying leaves;
a little-stegosaurus prowls
in the stench of primeval slime.

A basilisk in his own world,
gorging on newly-hatched tadpoles;
his orange belly and warty skin
warn of a foul taste –
a choke-skin suit of armour.

Night-prowler, he hides by day
from the terrible fire-stab-beak
whose shadow makes him shoot
beneath waterlily pads
into hornwort jungles.

Creature of two elements,
he waves his dinosaur tail
at his chosen one, beguiling
her with cologne
in his brightest spring suit.

Water-drake, in my hand
he is a slippery grenade –
he lies so still,
but like a thunderbolt
he's here . . . gone.

First published in Poetry Space's *Winter Showcase* 2017

Red Stag – Kate Innes

I crawl into the beamed hall of his chest,
cover myself in skin and fur and creep
to sleep in the stretch of the skull.

While shoulders hunch and narrow
into legs and cloven points,
blood gathers from watery pools
to its previous course. Muscle
binds to bone, and then – eyes open.
My new body rises from its resting place.

I shake my heavy head of winter branches
and taste the air with bared teeth.
The wound on my haunch grows hair,
frosted stiff brown-grey.
Breath clouds soften throat and lips.
Hooves test the rocky slope.

Clearing the stings, I fly, and bracken blurs.
I am Herne the Hunter and his quarry.
I know the smell only and the speed.
The past is a dream and before me lies
the incline of earth, the thinning canopy,
flowing into field and shielding hedge.

I know the sound and the strange,
hard ground, but no longer what it means.
Arrows of light cross the scent trail – and I am hit.
Twenty paces of shattered bone till
I lie down here – a flood of blood in my belly –
torn haunch, from which a buzzard rises.

Black Bear – Chrys Salt

Driving due north
we spot her on the verge
foraging for ants and dandelion,
no berries yet to fatten her.

She's cuddly, big as a human,
soft round ears erect,
button eyes sewn close
over a long furred snout.

She chomps and rummages
in lovage, fox-tail, plucks at
fireweed with prehensile lips -
then head askance and curious

lumbers towards our lay by
pads around the car.
snuffles the radiator,
headbutts the bonnet and peers in.

We're still as rabbits on a hill,
ears cocked for predators
in case a twitch of a hand or eye,
alerts her to our presence and alarms -

then she ambles off towards
the forest gloom, turns, glares at us,
humped, dangerous, claws glinting
like gang-land razors in the July sun.

Street performers – Rebecca Gethin

All she can do is follow, stick close
to the leader as if devoted, watch
every gesture so as to anticipate his intention
before every tug and jerk on the chain
attached to the ring in her nose.

Their mouth-smoke irritates her nose.
She smells whatever they're digesting.
Each of her hair follicles keeps watch
on their plans – she owes them for hot pokering
her nostrils and smashing her teeth and claws.

She's no longer a bear with teeth and claws
to fear, but a figure of fun,
standing up on her hind legs
like a furred mannequin. The first notes
on the fiddle are her cue to start jigging.

She's chained to this endless jigging
that he taught her by putting embers
under her paws so, by standing
on her back legs, she relieved the agony
in the fronts and learned to raise

one paw, then the other. She's raised
to her hind legs by melody.
A chain is attached to the wrist
of his bowing arm so as he plays faster
she cavorts faster. They think she loves *dancing*.

He says the flame drink makes her dancing
funnier because she's tipsy. He puts a hat
on her head and a bottle in her paws.
She can't rub her pelt against rough bark
or open her arse to the stars.

Her sleep is a cage. He calls her *Star*
but she won't answer. He owes her everything.
He says the ring he gave her shows devotion.

Note: Bears performed in London until the 1890s but were still being
used for this purpose in the 21st century in Spain and Eastern Europe
and notably at the World Cup in Russia, 2018.

Don't let them tell you they don't – Jane Burn

They're lying, you know, when they say that they don't
kill any more, for sport. I'm going to tell you
about the Village of the Badgers. This, I guarantee,
is the truth. Badgersville, we joked, my friend and I,
off down for a nosey, down the four-acre, catch
a loose pony, chase the odd stray cow. Lucky, once
in a while to pluck a treasure from the unkempt grass –
two beautiful skulls, gifted from natural deaths
and slowly chewed by time, bone-bleached by summers,
cleared by rain and cherished by me. Years, they've been there.
Decades. Pathways worn like village streets – down
to the stream to drink. Here and there, busy-busy,
seeking for food, blowing out cobwebs from burrowed sleep,
visiting the neighbours. Holes in the steep hillside.
It's very Watership Down, I have prosed, to fill
the bee-buzzed quiet. One, off with a basket,
to the mushroom fields. They have an out-of-date calendar,
pictures of roses pinned to the soil wall. My friend
rolls her eyes. It's her farm. She pretends to scorn
my highfalutin' speech. One day last autumn, just before
their horse and hounding season starts, they came on the sly,
on a work-day when most are away at the grind. Bent the wire
of the stock fence, clambering gang of tweedy men.
Shovelled the sets shut, put the terriers down. Lifted
the breathless bodies onto their quads, trophied them
across the handlebars. Drove away while my friend
stood nailed to the spot in fear and screamed.
You know us soppy folk. You pay no heed if your prey's
on private land. We don't understand your country ways.

Flightless – Isabelle Kenyon

They need to conquer the wildling
and display their skill on a perfectly plucked plate.

They need to tame their flight in cages;
kill their spirit before the fight.

They need to place a bullet securely
in the breastbone –
stop the ticker,
play the game,
survey the spoils:
delicious.

A Shift of Light – Alison Lock

The roe deer saw me, and I saw her.
We froze, her side eye encompassing the whole of me. We conversed
in a silent second, a dialogue of tension,
a tête-à-tête, where I was in awe of her, but for her, was I friend or foe?

Her beauty was in the sudden shift of light, the red-brown of her
still-summer coat, a grace among the dappled shades of autumn.

Before I could hold out my hand in peace, she leapt away, disappearing
into the forest. Leaving no tracks to prove my witness, but a fold
in my day had opened out like a notebook for me to write these words
– to share this moment with you.

The patron saint of hares – Mary Robinson
For Helen

I came to an open gateway
and at that same instant a hare entered
my field of vision. I am still. I am seeding grass,

brambles, nettles. She follows her known path,
a few steps at a time, pausing for scent
in the air, a tremor of earth beneath her feet.

When does she sense my presence?
                                      She halts
a shadow's length away. How quick she is
in her stillness, every hair of her pelt
pricked, every nerve taut as wire.

Which of us will break this moment?

I want the legend of the hare who hid
from the hunters under the skirts
of Saint Melangell at prayer to be true.

Respect – Corinne Lawrence

Mole - that's me.
Or, if you prefer, Mouldywarp – dirt tosser -
my name from time out of mind. Respect me.
My lifetime will be spent in the service of soil –
I am King of Crumble, Lord of Loam.

Earth is my obsession. Respect that.
Always I feel it flaked between my claws:
clods cling to my pallid palms.
Shovel-like, they are purpose built.

Relinquishing sight long ago,
I evolved an underground sat nav
second to none, am able to divine
the nearness of worms or infinitesimal
shifts of air where there is no air.
Worms respect me – fearful
of my paralysing saliva, of imprisonment
in my living larder. A neat touch,
don't you think?

Day and night do not exist
for me, though I relish the comfort
of snuggling into dirt-dark duvets,
will snooze happily under eiderdowns
of earth, or counterpanes of clay.

Above ground affairs don't concern me,
nor company entice me. Being alone suits me.
It's unlikely, but should you encounter a group of us,
we prefer to be addressed as 'a labour of moles' –
an appropriate acknowledgement of our industry.
A mark of respect, you might say.

Atlantic Grey – Susan Richardson

Skinny. Sticky with delivery.
Pink inch of umbilicus
    withering.
Mother whiskers his nose,
commits to mottled memory
his distinctive smell and cry.

Another pup, plump as summer
after two weeks' suckling, lunges
        for the teats
of his blubber-depleted mother,
her hips conspicuous as litter.

A skittish wind scatters
    tufts   of   white   fur
from an older moulter
whose mother has swum
into season, come-
       hithered   away to sea.

New pup sleeps, drenched
in the raw meat stench of fresh placenta
and what it's tempting to read as love.

A redshank lands on a perch
      of afterbirth,
beaks a scarlet strand
and starts to feast.

To Save a Butterfly – Lucinda Carey

First, notice the pulsating mud puddle
something is barely alive.
Waterlogged down, yet held afloat
by water tension.

Now is the heartbeat
in which to intervene, raise
the insect, support it beneath
with a strong short twig.

It is saved from immediate danger,
but it's soft powdery scales
furl limply round, sag and adhere
to the stick, it will die.

Having meddled in its plight
there is the butterfly-wing weight of
self-responsibility, fast decisions to make or
fear aroused panic will drip, rip and shred.

With serenity step into the sun,
let it evaporate the water.
Using the tiniest curve of white finger nail,
ease the wings up a fragment;

and exhale a gentle, a very gentle warm
breath, a breath of life, it's going to live!
It's almost at liberty, find a
sun-lit blackberry leaf and transfer carefully.

No longer in your hands, step away,
watch the wings fan out and un-darken,
become again iridescent.   It is a Red Admiral!
It is on the wing!

Fox – Gillian Prew

She serves the hill in all its gleaming gorse/ she
who fits with the land her clear self dazzling.

Her clear self
all blustery and buttery/ all stitched and sequined/ her cold mouth
bleeding/

her meeting
the wet wood
all woundweathered and hurting.

Keeps the hunt at bay/ keeps the blood-jackets from draining.
Holds her inner and outer reds, says that she is dying/

lying down the whole side of herself –
the grasses moaning the first ferns unfurling.

From *your verb is all water and light*

There Be Ligers And Tigons – Clive Donovan

He dreamt that he saw the buffalant. Thomas Hood the Younger

There be ligers and tigons living – did you know?
– offspring of two great cats – oh shock!
Are they sexual exiles? Are they shunned
or considered attractive freaks?
Oh scandalous genes! You have crossed boundaries:
Permitted to exist, but issue-less condemned to be,
as errant flowers shall your seed be halt
– pinched-off by evolution's stern decree.

But I would see rhinos chase poachers on puma legs,
elephant-monkeys take to trees,
lobbing nuts on ivory thieves!
and a cross of dragon-dodo shall, with nostril fire,
scorch all the sailors' looting boats
while songs of foxy mermaids in their dreadful game will snare
maddened hunters and their hounds to dark wet tombs,
alluring, as, on reddened rocks, they plait their long brown hair...

Blood Moon – Harry Owen

There's a blood moon drawing closer: the eclipse will have its say
For the word is that tomorrow's not the same as yesterday

I have looked into the eyes of Serengeti buffalo
And have felt their wildness hold me: I am dust bath, mud wallow
I am Ford, Mercedes, Kia, I'm Isuzu, Chevrolet
I'm the 4x4 Toyota man who's coming out to play
With the trophy buck, the kudu horn, the lion head, the gun
Chasing zebra, rhino, elephant where cheetah used to run
I'm a killer, I'm a sportsman, and I crave the pumping gore
Of my victims, whom I love, of course (I've told you this before)
For there's nowhere in the city's artificiality –
Concrete jungles, tarmac roadways, bricks and incivility –
That can see into my heart like this, can hold my blood in thrall
To the music of the wilderness: I am nothing, I am all,
I am gods and demons, Adam, Eve, the serpent, burning bush;
I am you and me and everything, I'm arid, I am lush
Yet I'm nothing, simply no one, in the vapid boardroom stink
Of cigars and empty jargon, of sales targets and the clink
Of worthless bits of shiny tin, wads of paper printed green,
The repulsive smirk, the groping hand, despicable, obscene
I am desperate to prove I'm not a failure, I'm not thick,
That my life has been worth living, but I find I'm just a dick

For this blood moon's drawing closer – an eclipse is on its way
And the fact is that tomorrow's just the same as yesterday

Office Outing – Annie Kedzlie

Factory-farmed pheasants plump and pumped
with meds, reared and released at last,
flee in fright as the first shots sound
from trigger-happy day-trippers
down from town to bond.
Bag the birds as beaters drive them
towards their deaths – forest floor littered,
let the wounded die where they lie.
The carnage is cleaned up later –
bury the birds or burn them,
too plentiful for the pot, not popular.
Bonded by bloodlust, the party dine on chicken
in a nice cream sauce for dinner.

The Racehorse – Emma Simmons

I am here.
They've brought me, I did not choose to come.
I did not want to be here, but I am.
I have no autonomy over my life.
I do not belong to me.

I stand.
They strap my face in leather from a cow who once lived.
They tie down my tongue and buckle my mouth shut.
It is hard to breathe, so tight it hurts.
I do not belong to me.

I am three years old.
My bones and joints still soft and forming
and yet they ride me. They beat me to run faster.
I must run, I must jump.
Even if it kills me.

It is time.
It jumps on my back. Light but hard and sharp.
They all are. It has a stick and it will hit me.
I know this. I must run, I must jump.
Even if it kills me.

Explosion.
We're off. We're free yet never more enslaved.
I try to run faster so they won't hit me
but it starts. It always does.
We do not matter.

Reality hits.
My friend has fallen.
His face plants into the earth, his bones break.
I cannot stop, I cannot help you, I am so sorry.
I must run, I must jump.

I feel the whip
hard on my hip. Again and again.
I want to go to my friend, to comfort him.
But I can't. I must run. I must jump.
I must - even if it kills me.

I see the flash of green
behind me as they cover his impending death.
I sense his agony, his terror. I hear the bullet
as if it were through my own skull.
As one day, it may be.

My friend.
You did not matter to them.
But you mattered to me. I couldn't stop,
I couldn't help you. I had to run, had to jump
Even though it killed you...

Dawn – Kayleigh Campbell

Frost blankets the early winter field.
The sky is crisp, cloudless.
A new mother surveys the scene;
no danger.
She calls her kits from their nest,
they bound over with springy, unsteady feet.
Ears upright, they form a chain
and meander over grass.
Button eyes glisten in the sun,
tails fluffier than the absent clouds.

Dancing Bear – Peter Geoffrey Paul Thompson

He dances comically to the crowd's delight.
Not in any ritzy nightclub,
but in rusty restraining chains
cutting into his red raw skin.

Perverse people clap and cheer, entertained,
as the menacing stick pokes him.
Money always wins in this poor land.
The nightly torture never ends in sleep.

Far from family, fed sparingly
(if he performs for the cheering crowd).
Fur matted by resting on his own urine
in a cramped cage

in a strange sweltering country,
his verdant forest home a distant memory.
He moves painfully to persistent drum beat,
the forced rhythms of the oppressed.

A furry, 'funny' clown,
prisoner of the 'noble' human race.
No trade union for animals,
his plaintive grunt of helplessness unheard

by cold greedy owners
like Victorian vampire bosses of northern mills,
sucking the blood out of him,
purses full of perspiration, pockets full of pain.

And tomorrow just another terrible time
of total torment...

A Brief Encounter – Janis Clark

I saw her on the brow of the hill.
A flash of fox among the ferns,
gold flecks of fur reflecting autumn sun.
I thought she would run but she stood unmoving,
her eyes fixed so firmly on mine
I could not look away.
Instead, I saw in her stare,
white teeth, stained red from frenzied hounds,
saliva-soaked hair on a mangled body,
a bloodied cheek of a first-time child,
and weakening cubs, still waiting.
I mouthed my silent apology
but there was neither fear nor forgiveness
as she turned into the cover of the trees.

Mid-March – Alison Brackenbury

Although the oak and ash spread bare
the buzzard's collar turns to snow.
Bedraggled in magnificence
pheasants, who hid from hushed guns, go.

Along the road – Alison Brackenbury

In Sussex, late
from the last bus
driving deep woods at night
I see the stag
trot headlamps' beam

rut in his blood
antlered by light.

'Along the road' published in *'The Rialto'*

Peekaboo Pangolin – Iulia David

*Inside a metal vault here in rural Vietnam is a creature believed to be the
most trafficked mammal in the world. No sounds come from its cage. No
squeaks or howls. CNN*

She uncovers the mound
as I watch ants like words
cloaked in her tongue,
sticky, a whip wiggling
up from below,
my body more tingly
as she shovels them down,
them blurred secrets
looming about alarmingly,
past the stout limbs, past
the bladelike jaw bone,
past the tube lips funnelling down,
fires upset from their beds,
rivers of them, entering
the plant of her gizzard,
where two pieces of grit
do the work for the day –
it is the mill hidden
in a shield so shy, past
the tapering snout, past
the bladelike jaw bone,
down in the scaly hoover,
there are rivers of them,
entering past where
humans grow the song
when we say her name:
pangolin, your name
tickly like a mandolin,
take the hands off my eyes

in broad white and I see
this question of you
thrown down from heaven –
what sort of scaffolded dream
are you. As I watch,
the answer comes,
a rattle with no sound –
Peekaboo pangolin!
Now we see you;
now we don't.
Down there,
past the vicious air,
past the scare,
hiding your muscle
in the concord of nails,
past memory,
nocturnal,
curling up,
toothless
and almost blind:
play dead.
Play dead.
Play dead.

High Park Zoo Capybaras Escape! – Barbara Barnes

the chase is on as Bonnie and Clyde go on the lam

You will not find us.
Our dip-dyed russety pelts meld
into autumn's fallen flooring.

Clever jays find us, sparrows too,
our foreheads their sleek settees.
We are not the armed escapees

you hunt for. Our fearsome incisors
drip green as we lunch on
salad selections, our dog's bark

has no bite. Afternoons we are
hippos lolling in the pond,
currents roll our barrel bodies.

Truth be told we loved our unnatural home; llamas in spitting
distance, the emu opposite

legging it. Doing time we doubled
our years, safe from leopard death.
But who would not roam

if roaming were an option?
Misguided posse, call off the search.
Look for the hole in your fence.

From news story *Toronto Star*

The birdsong has gone – Brian Blackwell

The birdsong has gone

The meadows by Manston Lane
were so tranquil, so fulfilling,
voluptuous with wildlife.

I once nearly stood on a nest
of eggs quite close to a curlew
with its desperate wail.

Nearby a flock of peewits, forever
in a flap that hardly helped them to fly.
Then there were the trills of the skylarks

ascending as skylarks do, then silently plop
to their land-based brood, where the peewits
lapwinged out of sync with their goals.

Now they have gone. A motorway extension,
its slip roads, the lorries with their countless tons
of rock, of concrete, tarmac, exhaust fumes.

Just synthetic noise and dust. A totally different
smell. No tranquillity; no rural fragrance.
No birdsong. The birdsong has gone.

Manston Lane is within the city boundary of Leeds, West Yorkshire.

The Lion's Pride – Carolyn O'Connell

He roamed the savannah camouflaged
against gold grasses, ancient trees
his head surrounded by a main of hair,
a crown proclaiming supremacy.

His pride attracted the European hunters
equal to their conquests of Empires.
His head, and those of others,
adorned hunters' halls of England.

Symbols of power of man and beast
their dusty heads lingered:
deer, elephant, badger, rhino –
the Trophies of an Empire
we thought had been freed.

No! Planes drop wealthy scions
deep in the African 'canned parks'
armed, ready to hunt lions
taught not to run as cubs –

for tourists have stroked them,
petted them like kittens, now
they lack fear of man, a natural instinct.
Slowly the Savannah empties –

the great beasts are going!
Africa has lost its heritage;
the right of the lion to live
the right of the human to live.

What glory a "Trophy" culled from the tamed?

Feel Time – Pauline Hawkesworth

Fish-down on holly grass,
lost in frozen seas,
really thought you had
caught me out, cut through
the frigidness on scaly-skin.

Now it's feel time, melt time,
hot-rod on the holly time;

it was pheasants hung on a broken
washing line, feathers on grass,
time caught on bards – that is how
I saw them – heads twisted,
somewhere there is a man in these hills
vicious as a crocodile.

Peregrine – Jane Lovell

He has found her,
courts her with precise spirals:

rolls, unpinned, folds, falls
through fractured air,

gives her the whole sky streaming
with birds,
wind-riven cliffs,
the bay, its cobbled maps of flint.

Implicit in his sleight and sweep,
the headlong stoop:
ferocity and fearlessness, intent.

He takes in every pulse and flicker,
drift of gull and soaring raven,
marks them,
        gauges probability,
calculates his own dark energy
        then he's gone,
sprung from steel, atomic.

Every bone and blade of him is free.

He has his own agenda,
his own skewed symmetry
        of slate and flint,
the disarticulated skeletons
of snakes and fish,
perfect whorls of ammonite.

See him rise and arc across a land
unfixed by frosts,
the transience of chalk,
its pools of windblown light.

Guy Fawkes Geese – Karen Jane Cannon

The sky explodes—
a million pieces of light
rim the bowl of hills.

Suddenly—the geese circling Daer reservoir
trying to land. They've flown far reaches
of arctic chill, to stop and rest feather-map wings
as the world blows apart.

A rocket soars, another—with every bang we hear them
rise and call above Glengonnar weather station,
a reflected chaos of light and geese, echoing
round the Lowthers.

This is not the raw call of spring flights,
beating of wings, stretching with the need to fly.
This—the wild *honk! honk! honk!* of a journey
impossible to complete.

They have circumnavigated blasted slicks of North Sea oil,
gun barrels trained over Cromarty Firth,
bodies twisting through invisible lines of static, arcing
power cables with *Caution!* signs. Once birds dropped dead
as they flew over this village, asphyxiated
by noxious lead fumes.
But now—

Each spark is a feather softly drifting to earth—
I want to catch each spark and make a coat of light,
guide the geese safely on their flight south.

Pheasant roulette – Pat Edwards

Five shots ring out,
each a maiming or a death.

Soft-mouthed dogs
became loyal bearers.

Lead shot bouncing round the wheel,
from black to red to dead.

I think of pheasants,
awkward at take-off into flight.

I think of shooters
knocking back shots from flasks.

I think this is no game,
only black to red to dead.

Placid landscape – Miriam Calleja

line up the trees
place the crunch of rocks
steady them as you go
sprinkle sand and soil
shake the foundation
make sure everything has settled
let the birds free
set the squirrels to roam
unleash the wild cats
coax the bears out
(promise them honey)
gentle now with the bees
plead with the praying mantises
recreate some fog with a machine
and let it all be quiet
look at the paradise you've made
then let it get lost in a fire

Trophy – Natalie Scott

He's the perfect specimen:
devoted partner, father of two.
Takes care of the family pride.
An Oscar winner. No, the Oscar
itself. Tall, muscular, pure-gold.

He can be lazy, yes, but no more
than other males, and females,
well, they like preparing his meals.
In return he will fight for them
till the death. That's the deal.

He's the perfect specimen
of his kind, and that makes him
a relic. Not to be loved, honoured,
treasured. No. To be hunted,
collected. Kept. His prowess

squeezed into jars, so that
others may own a piece of him,
be more like him. You see, they
are excruciatingly weak. So weak
that they cannot shoot straight.

He's so strong it takes him
two days to die. Naked, alone,
in pain. This fine human specimen,
devoted husband, father of two,
with his beautiful lion's mane.

Eviction Notice – Marilyn A Timms

Pheasants have done really well this year.
Hoping for a record kill next month.
So, can't have Reynard filching a few
for his breakfast, spoiling our chances,
can we? Foxy gotta go.
Give the guns a sporting chance!

Ever ridden to hounds? Bloody marvellous!
Best day of my life when I got bloodied.
Forty years on, though, and Foxy's still here.
Trouble with hunting, you can't be sure
of a kill. We've tried boarding up the earths.
Damned hard work and half the time

the little buggers slip away through
a back door. No, what you want is a snare.
Application of art and science, match cunning
with cunning. Twenty snares, five days,
and you've got a fox, guaranteed. Here;
wrap your eyes around this beauty.

Legit? Course it's legit. Trust me!
Even got a Defra code of practice.
They say *approach trapped fox downwind*
and despatch with a shotgun while it's sitting calmly.
Chance'd be a fine thing! And if Foxy gets caught
round the middle, well, he'll thresh all over the place.

One thing I must tell you. Remember this!
Once you've pulled the carcase out of the snare,
never go and check another one. You'll stink of fox.

It will transfer to anything else you touch.
Foxy will smell it on the trap and stop and sniff it,
get distracted, and pop off in another direction.

Always carry water and un-perfumed soap in the car,
give yourself a sporting chance!
Non-target catches? Inevitable. Hey, life's a gamble!
They didn't have to walk into my snare. Had 'em all!
Rabbits, hare, deer. Even had an otter once.
Beautiful he was. Dead, of course. But beautiful.

You can't shoot non-targets unless they're injured
and it's the only humane thing to do. Wire-cutter job!
You'll get prosecuted if they die or live, either way,
so keep stum about it. We're supposed to check snares
at least once in 24 hours but when there's heavy rain,
cold beer, and a hot woman, what would you do?

The dog was the worst. No idea what it was doing
on private property in the first place. Tore itself free
and left a mess of muscle and fur behind. Still, he chases
a ball on three legs, seems happy enough. Result!
It's owner's kicking up a stink, though, wants to sue.
Damned unsporting, don't you think?

St Kevin and the Blackbird – Seamus Heaney

And then there was St Kevin and the blackbird.
The saint is kneeling, arms stretched out, inside
His cell, but the cell is narrow, so
One turned-up palm is out the window, stiff
As a crossbeam, when a blackbird lands
And lays in it and settles down to nest.
Kevin feels the warm eggs, the small breast, the tucked
Neat head and claws and, finding himself linked
Into the network of eternal life,
Is moved to pity: now he must hold his hand
Like a branch out in the sun and rain for weeks
Until the young are hatched and fledged and flown.
*

And since the whole thing's imagined anyhow,
Imagine being Kevin. Which is he?
Self-forgetful or in agony all the time
From the neck on out down through his hurting forearms?
Are his fingers sleeping? Does he still feel his knees?
Or has the shut-eyed blank of underearth
Crept up through him? Is there distance in his head?
Alone and mirrored clear in love's deep river,
'To labour and not to seek reward,' he prays,
A prayer his body makes entirely
For he has forgotten self, forgotten bird
And on the riverbank forgotten the river's name.

From *The Spirit Level,* 1996 Reprinted with permission Faber and Faber

St Kevin's Gift – Nicola Warwick

Don't be put off by this;
it isn't meant to test
or harm you. Think of it
as a step in evolution,
like archaeopteryx
when it first risked a flight.

Don't worry that you're not as clever
as crow. You have his dark back,
a more seductive song,
golden-ringed eyes
and a beak as rich in colour
as egg yolk.
You will puzzle it out,
weigh the task in your head,
your fine brain measuring the span
between branch and food,
working out how much your spine
can flex, your feet can hold.

Yes - a rush of black,
a leap, wings a-thrum
in the tree, a peck, a stab,
beak snatching the food,
crumbs falling like
Manna from heaven.

Collateral Damage – Pamela Trudie Hodge

Dusk
and along the riverbank
an undulating hunter ripples
through reed and Himalayan Balsam.

Alien. Imported for trade,
decimator of water voles,
his ancestors broke free
from cage and wire,
colonised waterways
leaving behind half a century
of moorhen feathers,
the string tails of voles,
traces of crunched bone in their scat.

Sharp teeth honed,
blood-spattered pelage river-washed,
smoothed with a swift tongue.

Self-consciously she smooths
the pelt of her mink coat.
bought years ago
by an elderly lover
with more cash than virility.

Uncaring. Unthinking.
A remote killer teetering
on four inch heels.

White Rhino in Winter – Jan Moran Neil

And suddenly ... clamped on road side,
zooless, but ours for the viewing,
prehistoric pedestrian, pavement slab for hide,
blank blinkers stare seemingly, at nothing.

Handicapped horn bent towards winter earth,
the haunting whisper of captivated guide,
'She carried two calves for fourteen months.
She lost them last week to a pride.'

Mother's eyes on sun drenched winter evening.
Weighted monument in mourning.

Wolf Watch – Susan Taylor

An amber eye into the past, half a face
appears from out of the trunk of an evergreen;
surrogate branch with a single ochre leaf
from entirely different stock,
surrounding pelt, bristly as needles.

Sharp need to keep an eye out,
ghosting a fifty stride length ahead,
there again, same distance behind.

Traveller through the forest,
you always have a companion,
a watcher with light set deep in the black
in the thorn in the iris in the eye.

You have a chance to be held there,
part of this knowledge,
ancient woodcraft, padding through twig litter
without snap of a sound,
so bird never gets into flap
or releases slight twink of alarm from throat.

This is the trick of soft fur
pushing through cushions of pads,
roundels of auburn plush, tipped
with minute adjustments of claws dark polish.

Intrigue of delicate bones tunes
a balancing act, mysterious as unit of wind
moving through trees,
fluid among them, quiver of nose

pivots on an arrow of scent,
heady and strong
as music of hoof-fall to follow.

It ghosts you, flawless apparition,
you are a single thread
in the beam of an eye.

It knows our type,
remembers what we once were,
at one with the wood, but now,
one of many who take it for granted,
not to run with the pack,
or be part of this melting away.

We think we may have imagined
the brazen god-like eye,
a bead of sunlight left in its place
as socket for eye to slot into.
Such is ever the vision of trees, so much
dismembered here, so many lives gone.

Marriage – Susannah Violette

the fort gives us its rings
the oak too
I will marry you here
beneath this tilled sky
seeded with leaves

your fur is autumn
arriving through falling
the wheel turns

your teats give up nitrates
their death-milk miasma
a confetti of flies make this a wedding
you dear dead fox, smile
for the wetness of the rain

your corpse, so full of having lived
the rose-hip of your still heart
itches at its browning centre

beloved, I will marry you
here in the dead grasses
beside this Roman road

Intrusion – Sam Smith

Where fallen catkins lie like waterlogged maggots
and squared rocks attract fern and moss
on a spinney floor, among black ivy, hunts
a translucent spider with long delicate legs
like an out-of-water prawn

In among a nest of roots
goes a belly-slithering rat
slyness the heart of his survival

Under a slate-scratched sky starlings probe fields
with long sharp beaks. Woodpigeons
in hedgerow hawthorns
are beginning to build their perilous nests of twigs
Rabbits, colour of dried dung, are mounds quick to kick
demonstrate the wise fear they have of my kind

Hawk, jackdaw, crow
wings flat and folded back
drop like spent ballistics

One grey helicopter in the grey distance floats
light as ash, a semi-transparent midge. Here
nature, piece to piece, life to life, fits.
And here, hooves clattering, they come
those who dress in pink and call themselves hunters
hooligans on horseback blowing bugles

Re-Naming the Hare – Mandy Pannett

Hare, a staccato name for one whose nature
shifts with the measures of time.

Precious to Aphrodite, you are a moonlight myth.
A gift to be offered in love.

As star, you are *Lepus*, south of Orion's Hunt.
Always the quarry, poised to leap –

see how carefully they've threaded you
through tapestry's woodland groves. Your long ears

listen for hounds and horn.

Tiney, Puss, Bess, Cowper named
his three pet hares his comforters

against depression, furry guards at suicide's gate.

Tiney, his favourite, nibbler of twigs and the cucumber vine,
if made to sit on a lap, would drum on his owner's knees.

'I pledge myself to protect the hare' the poet said, 'with all
that is human in me'. Compassion was in you, Cowper –

unlike those who relish pain, will shoot and snare and watch
as a screaming hare is ripped in two by bloody jaws.

Hare, for me you are silence, the *sittestille* I saw one winter dawn
in a field of frost; wide-eyed and ready to run.

Arctic Fox – Stephen Bone

For decades it must have hung –
this last relic of her vanity –
like an unwanted rescue dog
in her wardrobe's mothballed cave.
Room to breathe, the Danish furrier had said.

Burlesquely I wrap myself in its embrace,
feel an almost living warmth, dark hint
of an Arctic summer running through
the narrow head and back.

A stale whisper of its perfumed history,
returning her in Kodak colour
sipping Fernet Branca on Alpine terraces
or promenading Cunard decks. Mouth full-blown
with Victory Red; amber eyes like set traps.

First published in *The Poetry Shed* and *In The Cinema,* Playdead Press
2014

Brasside Ponds – Rachel Burns

The cormorants sit stock still
perched like garden ornaments on sunken trees.
Everywhere there are warning signs
>   *Private Land*
>   *Shooting in this area.*

The lake is filled with bricks and broken glass.
Coots call out harsh unmusical notes
the sound like a hammer
tap, tap, tap on a sheet of metal.

A high security prison overshadows the water.
The inmates walk around the exercise yard
as wild geese fly in a V or straight-line skein
honking *aang- ang- ang* in the sky.

Every day an elderly couple collect
stale bread from the local supermarket
bring it to the lake in carrier bags.

I think that bread is bad for ducks.
Once walking with my toddler children
around the ponds, a huntsman fired a warning shot
over my head, over my children's heads.

I closed my eyes, fear tore through me
the split second of all-encompassing dread
that I might be killed
that my children might be killed.

My children are older now
both at school and I still walk around the two lakes
skirting the path in a figure of eight, ignoring the warning signs.
In the centre of the lake, the cormorants wait.

In remembrance of hares – Tina Negus

We are drawing hares, thirty-odd assorted members
of three art groups, being taught a new technique:
pastel painting on velour paper.
I am pleased with the result, though doubt it is really
the medium of choice, for me.

Memories return of hares, running, jumping, fighting
on the Downs, in frosted furrows, mad March hares indeed.
And hares following their labyrinthine ways, criss-crossing
the ancestral routes of badger, fox and roe deer, high on the hill,
the various high-ways marked by a darker twisting strip of grass,
flattened foliage, nibbled herbs, a trodden path, linking
gaps through limestone walls, burrows, forms, latrines…

Soft pastel clogs the furred surface, is rubbed smooth
with a grimy finger, the colour intensified, layer by chalky layer,
building the picture, defining the form.

I remember the hare running towards us, on our ancient track,
the green lane, the drovers' road, the Long Hollow.
Wild-eyed in fright, he was fleeing the approaching dog, unaware
of our presence until he was almost at our feet, my camera
forgotten in the excitement of the moment.
Like a cartoon animal, it screeched to a halt, fore-paws braced,
jinxed, darted through the hedge, and raced off over the field,
leaving the dog panting in frustration.

The painting takes shape, blocking-in darks, mid-tones, lighter areas,
each application of colour blended into the whole, a limited palette,
                                        black, mid-brown,
ochre, ivory, figuring the texture of grizzled fur,

revealing the light falling on muzzle, crown, laid-back ear.

I see again the farm trailer, waiting by the gate, the men smoking,
                                        guns broken,
the laid-out lines of the newly-dead, with eyes clouded in death,
                                        limbs limp in death,
lips drawn back exposing curving yellowed teeth in death...
Judge and jury, executors and executed, found guilty of grazing
on winter wheat, paying the price.

It is time to add the finishing detail to the drawing: we are allowed
                                        at last
a stick of hard white pastel, to delineate the whiskers, and finally
the eye, the golden iris, the oval pupil, reflecting the sunlight, the open
                                        sky,
the wildness of place, the freedom of life.

Awarded 1st place in Quantum Leap Open Competition Autumn 2014and
published in QL 68, Nov 2014.
Read on *Radio Bute fm by Alan Carter on Dec 27th 2014.*

Silent Fox – Vivien Jones

If needs be, I am silent.
Behind, beneath this mesh
of brambles, I wait,
trembling just a little,
on this frosty morning.

I sense the dogs and horses
through the ground,
smell their sweat, their dung,
know it not much different
than my own,

and a sharper vile scent,
a smell outside nature.
The riders are not silent
but sound their gleeful horns
as they come closer.

I whimper, I void myself,
should I run, should I stay ?
A single hound lifts his nose,
sifts the air, scents me, barks,
the others turn their heads.

Then it is thunder, it is a storm
of hooves galloping this way,
I can see the tails of many hounds,
scything the air; they are close,
they are too close for flight.

If needs be, if these brambles
are torn apart, before the hounds
and their snapping jaws,
I will unlock my throat
to announce my end.

Corvus Marinus – Sheena Bradley

Tarred with the same satanic brush as Raven,
the cormorant has been cursed,
branded gluttonous and ugly.
       He trudges thick-ankled over shingle,
webbed feet slop as he lurches
spread-eagled from rock to rock
in search of colourful seaweed
to beautify the nest.

No song to enrapture a poetic heart,
his stuttering croaks echo
from barren cliffs where he huddles
gossiping low and amicable
with other craggy silhouettes,
  or perches high on a lifeless tree
to guard his fledglings with piercing cries.

But watch when he dives from a height
with iridescent wings pulled tight to chest,
elongated beak, neck and body a lethal dart
of dignity and poise,
cleaves the water and disappears.

In time the cormorant bursts forth,
a wriggling fish clenched in his beak,
disposed of with a noble flick
and swallowed whole,
precise and dextrous in the execution.

Watch him
spread his wings,

balance
in crucifixion pose
to dry the feathers and warm
the breast -
and say he is unholy.

A 'Poem of the Year' winner – Reach Poetry, Indigo Dreams

Fox Cub and Vixen – Veronica Aaronson

And there he is
in the morning brightness –
ginger fur,
hunting nose to the ground.

We meet eye to eye,
not daring to blink,
six feet held as if in wet clay,
mouths ajar.

Then our silence
is cut by vixen yelp,
yapping of frenzied hounds,
vixen scream.

Cumulus covers sun.

He turns to go,
looks back,

I feel his eyes
and her scream
being fired in the kiln
of my body.

Hunter – Pete Brown

The gun is just fun
You can kill
Dumb creatures
One by one
They don't really mind
They're not humankind
How can you call me scum?

Into The Blue Sky – Miki Byrne

(Foot & mouth epidemic. 2001. Grand Union Canal)

On a slow canal by silent fields,
a boat lay captive.
Yellow tape defined a corral alongside it.
Closed towpath access, curtailed all freedoms.
A sign shouted threat of contagion,
that closed waterways, chained locks,
denied the boat-dweller all amenities
and a place to walk two bounding dogs.
The towpath bristled, incongruously golden
under disinfectant-soaked straw, that spiked
bright tangles underfoot.
Mingled sharp stench with the dark choke
of smoke and burned flesh.
It soaked like damp into every breath.
Seeped into clothes
Brought a sense that civilisation had ended.
Left few to survive and brought silence
to the land.
The boat-dweller, fretted against confinement.
Grieved for a tragedy of vast proportion.
Watched distant pyres smoke souls
of hoofed beasts, into a clear blue sky.

Death of a Hind – Lynne Munn

Cold, pale February
The hunt is thundering by,
Sad, grey morning
The hind will die.

Wild cry of terror
Borne on the wind,
Oh! see where the bracken
Is stained with blood.

All winter long
Safe and warm,
She carried the calf
That now is torn...

Torn...torn...
Out of the gaping wounds,
And with her entrails garlanded
Fed to the ravaging hounds.

A walk in Spencer's wood – Mark Haworth-Booth

Are you guarding a new cache of nuts for winter?
You're surely old enough to know that I'm a threat.

You come pouncing along a fallen branch –
each move you make too quick for me to see.

Only your tail moves slowly: you shape it
in bows and arcs – I think they're meant for me

but you've sprung to the bole of a beech and flattened
yourself to the bark with your tail topmost

signalling: three quivers ripple your full-
stretched plume – and then a pause and now three more

a pause and then three more – like semaphore
waved in the face of a dim-witted giant.

I guess you're saying *I am here* and *mine*
and start to gesture back *please stay, I'll go*

but quicker than thought you disappear –
leaving a sense of kinship in the air.

One Morning in September – Ronnie Goodyer

"When they first told me about this, I didn't believe them.
I just couldn't believe anyone could be so cruel.
To set a pack of dogs on fox cubs – how could they?"

The vixen has done well, her four cubs are thriving.
For six months they have bonded, played and grown
almost to maturity, fine red-brown coat and black boots.
Soon they will be leaving to start their own families.

> The hunt slows and holds up, circling a copse.
> Whips strike saddles, sounds turn the morning cold.
> The vixen sniffs the air, knows something is wrong.
> She barks. Young hounds run in to learn their purpose.

All has changed. The terrified cubs home now their death-trap.
They bolt in fear but are driven back by shouts and screams,
noise they've never experienced and will never hear again.
In pain, they are caught with jaws, mauled and ripped apart.

> Trotting back, they all agree it was a perfect, gentle day,
> great exercise for the horses, and a valuable social occasion.
> Late into the day, a cautious vixen investigates her home.
> It is empty. It smells of blood. And it is so very silent...

"Sport? It's pure evil slaughter for fun, that's what it is.
People should know about this – help these animals.
Someone should speak up For The Silent."

INDEX

Indigo Dreams Publishing
24 Forest Houses
Halwill
Beaworthy
Devon
EX21 5UU